WHAT OTHERS ARE SAY] NETWORKING

As a fellow networking expert who has spoken about networking for over a decade, written a book on the topic, and presented a TEDx as well, I found great value in reading *High Level Networking*. I enjoyed how practical this book is with great stories to illustrate key points. It was clarifying to hear how power partners are different from raving fans, and I'm excited to implement my own Follow Up Friday habit. I would recommend this book for entrepreneurs who already feel comfortable networking and are looking for a way to take it to the next level.

- **Robbie Samuels**, Author of *Small List, Big Results* and *Croissants vs. Bagels,* **RobbieSamuels.com**

High Level Networking is a gift to business owners. With over 15 years of networking experience, no one teaches like Terilee Harrison. One of her special gifts is helping you see things bigger and clearly communicate with your networking partners what connections and resources you need most to move the needle in your business. Get the book! Read it! Use it! Share it!

- **Chella Diaz**, Pricing Wizard, **ChellaDiaz.com**

If you want super success then you need to be a super connector, and this book will teach you what you need to know!

- **David T. Fagan**, Beverly Hills Talent Agent, **DavidTFagan.com**

High Level Networking is a must read for any business owner interested in building their business through referrals and relationships. Terilee Harrison teaches strategies to help you grow your business with ease.

- **Tobin Slaven**, Entrepreneur and School Founder, **TobinSlaven.com, ActonAcademy.com**

High Level Networking by Terilee Harrison is the roadmap that will allow you to create a steady stream of referrals. It's packed with guidance and practice advice you can immediately implement no matter what industry you're in. Love her work!

> **- Edward Zia,** International Master Influencer Coach,
> **EdwardZia.com**

When it comes to networking, if Terilee Harrison isn't doing it, then it's not worth doing. She's a master in the online world which we've all come to navigate over these past two years. I have had the pleasure of virtually meeting and knowing Terilee since late 2020 through the Virtual TEAM Community. Terilee is the master networker. She is a connector and collaborator and provides many opportunities for others to learn and participate. Her coaching has helped many in my network. She always encourages everyone to reach for their Big ASK. This book will take your networking to the next level.

> **- Dhea Bartlett,** Founder of Dhea's Ideas & BWIB Women
> Networking, Executive with Greener Still/SendOutCards,
> **dheabartlett.com**

Foreword by **ERIC LOFHOLM**

Author of *Continuous Sales Improvement*

HIGH LEVEL NETWORKING

Strategies to Expand Your Network,
Build Referral Relationships and
Joint Venture Partnerships,
and Grow Your Email List

TERILEE HARRISON

High Level Networking

Strategies to Expand Your Network, Build Referral Relationships and Joint Venture Partnerships, and Grow Your Email List

Foreword by Eric Lofholm

Edited by Terry L. Harrison

Cover design by Armend Meha

Interior design by Blessing

Download the *High Level Networking Vault* (for FREE)!

READ THIS FIRST.

To help you implement the strategies in this book, I've created worksheets and resources for you. Download them all at no cost in the *High Level Networking Vault.*

Best,

Terilee Harrison

Go to *www.highlevelnetworkingbook.com/vault* to gain access now.

TABLE OF CONTENTS

DEDICATION

For HGH and "Baby H". Your lives were meant to shine.

FOREWORD

By Eric Lofholm

Terilee Harrison loves serving people. She loves to share her gifts to help people step into their potential!

In her career working with thousands of business owners, Terilee has focused on how to become an elite networker and then how to teach others how to do the same. In *High Level Networking*, she shares her proven formulas on how to show up powerfully when you network.

Terilee's ideas are so much more than just networking at events. She shares how to leverage your connections to create a steady stream of referrals, how to create joint venture partnerships to build the business of your dreams, and how to build your email list and increase your follow up efforts. Your email list can be the #1 asset in your business. This one concept alone can be a game changer for you!

I have committed my life's work to teaching proven sales principles to help salespeople and sales teams increase their sales results. When you combine sales training and the networking concepts Terilee teaches, you will be unstoppable in your business!

The best advice I could give you is to read *High Level Networking* and apply these ideas. Make a decision right now that you will read the book until you have completed it, and then take every great idea you learn in this book and apply it to your business.

When you apply Terilee's ideas, you will achieve all of your networking goals.

Eric Lofholm

Eric Lofholm International

INTRODUCTION

Ask yourself if what you are doing today is getting you closer to where you want to be tomorrow. — Unknown

The truth is ... I was too afraid to attend my first business mixer.

I remember I could see the mixer attendees mingling in the courtyard of the venue as I pulled my car into the parking lot of the shopping plaza where the event was located. Even though I pretty much knew what to say, where to place my name badge, how to properly shake hands and more, I did not have the confidence to professionally represent myself and begin building business relationships. *What if someone asked me something I didn't know the answer to?*

I didn't have the guts to walk in that night.

I remember I didn't even bother to park my car. I called my husband from the parking lot that night saying, "I'm coming home. I'll go next month."

When I first left the corporate world and began being responsible for my own success in 2005, I understood that networking was important to my success. But I had no idea what I was doing and when I began attending networking events soon after, I got off to a really, slow, start.

Here's the problem: they don't teach us networking in school. Yet networking is one of the most important skills that anyone can have—no matter what you do for a living!

Yet ask yourself these questions to see if you have experienced what I have experienced:

Are you new to networking in general and don't know where to start?

Or have you been networking for a while and don't feel your efforts are paying off in a meaningful way?

1

Or maybe you love networking and would like to create a steady stream of referrals?

If you're like me, you've seen "it's not what you know, but who you know" play out in your life again and again.

So, why don't they teach networking in school?

Have you ever thought that networking doesn't work? I'm sure we've all been there. When you feel like this, I invite you to look in the mirror. Ask yourself if you've been showing up and giving your absolute all for your networking partners. And ask yourself, have you been playing BIG or thinking small?

Do any of these networking results sound familiar?

You "wing it" in your one-minute commercial – if you even have a one-minute commercial – and, of course, it gives you "wing it" results – not much if anything.

You spend hours networking attempting to reach more people— but then you don't follow up.

You want to collaborate with other business owners, but don't know where to start.

You worry where your next customer is coming from.

If you resonate with any of the above results, keep reading. Networking works when you know how to work it. If your business is not where you want it to be, you need to reach more of the right people. It's a fact: the more you network, the more business owners you connect with, the more money you can make.

Throughout *High Level Networking*, I will share step-by-step how you can receive a steady stream of introductions and referrals and how to:

⊙ Expand your network.

⊙ Build referral relationships.

- Collaborate with power partners and create joint venture partnerships.

- Build your email list.

- And pull it altogether in a Networking Success Blueprint.

To your success,

Terilee Harrison

A STARTING POINT: TAKE THE *HIGH LEVEL NETWORKING* ASSESSMENT

As you are beginning to learn the strategies of *High-Level Networking*, now is a perfect time to assess your current networking efforts. This assessment will help you determine any areas where you can improve. Getting "real" about where you are now can help you move forward to create a steady stream of referrals! Be open to level up your networking activities.

If you are experiencing challenges in your networking, it can be easy to blame your networking partners (*they* don't get me!) or your networking organization (*this* isn't working for me!)

But when was the last time you examined your own efforts and asked what you can do to improve the situation? We are all busy in the daily activities of running our business, and I bet it's been a long time (or possibly never) that you thought about improvements you can make in your networking efforts! Good news! Today's the day you can get real about your networking.

When you look at the *High Level Networking* Assessment, be honest with yourself in your responses.

As you read each of the items, rate yourself on a scale of 1 to 10, with 1 "I need serious help in this area!" and 10 being "I can't do any better. I've got this down!"

After you finish rating yourself in each area, add up all your points (there can be no more than 100 points.)

Question One: Maximizing Participation in Your Networking Groups

Do you attend as many networking events as possible?

Are you intentional in how you show up to network?

Do you focus on building relationships with (not selling to) other professionals?

Do you strive to be present with your networking partners – really paying attention to what they're saying and what their business needs are?

Do you maximize all benefits that are offered in the networking groups you're part of such as online trainings, directories or more?

_____ I maximize my participation in all the networking groups I'm part of.

Question Two: Communicating with Your One Minute Commercial

Are your One Minute Commercials always understood—meaning do you get the introductions and referrals you are looking for?

_____ I always give a One Minute Commercial other networkers can clearly understand.

Question Three: Making the Big ASK

When you share what you do with your business, do you always ask your networking partners for what you need next in your business (like a connection or a resource)?

Do you level up your ask to help you reach your goals even faster? (For example: I have a new program launching. I like to be a guest on business podcasts, etc. I'm looking for people who can help me do this.)

_____ I always share a Big ASK.

Question Four: Follow-up One-to-Ones

Do you consistently meet with new professionals and feel comfortable connecting and building relationships with them that could lead to referrals?

Are you intentional in how you show up to one-to-ones?

_____ I feel confident in the art of holding effective, productive one-to-one sessions.

Question Five: Connecting Through Your Business Presentations

When you present your business, do you regularly have audience members reach out to you with interest in getting to know you better as a potential referral partner, to request your lead magnet, or book a complimentary consultation?

_____ The business presentations I give always prompt many people to connect with me.

Question Six: Working with Your Power Partners

Do you know what types of businesses synergistically work well with yours because you serve the same client, but in different ways? (I call these business owners your "power partners").

Do you spend 80%+ of your networking time with your power partners?

Do you hold back from reaching out to new power partners because you lack confidence?

_____ I consistently seek out and build new Power Partner relationships.

Question Seven: Focus on Joint Venture Partner Relationships

Do you allocate some of your networking time focusing on creating and leveraging joint venture partner relationships where they promote you to their list and you promote them in return?

_____ I spend time developing and growing Joint Venture Partnerships.

Question Eight: Growing an Email List

Do you have an email list?

Are you growing your list with intention or are your contacts in chaos?

_____ I am actively growing my email list.

Question Nine: Your Follow Up

Do you stay on top of your follow up?

Or do you drop the ball and are your connections "in chaos"?

_____ I have a follow up plan in place that works extremely well for me.

Question Ten: Plan Your Networking Activities

At the start of each month, do you ask yourself…

- ◉ *What are my goals?*
- ◉ *Where will I network?*
- ◉ *How many new connections will I reach out to this month?*
- ◉ *What will I ask my networking partners for?*

_____ I strategically plan my networking activities each month.

GRAND TOTAL _____

As you look at these statements, what comes up for you? Did you find you had several low numbers? If you did, you are in good company. No one has ever scored 100.

The good news is no matter how you rated; you are in the right place at the right time because we will be focusing on leveling up in all these areas throughout this book.

Before you read any further, pause to examine how important it is to tie your networking strategy to your business goal setting. Considering your business goals when developing your networking strategy can help you create a steady stream of referrals. Here are three reasons why:

First, to grow, you need to get out of your comfort zone and take different actions than you have in the past. When you are clear on your goals, it can push you to do the things you don't want to do -- even when you don't feel like it.

Second, sharing your goals with your networking partners is powerful. For example, when you share, "I want to retire my wife and bring her home," it shows your networking partners what's important to you now and they will want to help you!

Last, when you ask your networking partners for what you need, you will ask with intention --focusing on what you need to reach your goals.

So, let's get clear by lasering your focus on your goals and declaring your intentions:

Get clear in a positive focus. *What is your big goal for the next 90 days? Or the next year? When you achieve this goal, what will it mean to you?*

Commit to a length of time for working with this intention. *I will do XX for the next 90 days or I will do XX for the next year.*

Recommit to your intention daily. *At the start of each day, remind yourself of your intention.*

Let your intention teach you by checking in throughout the day by asking, *Is what I'm doing now bringing me closer to my goals?*

Visualization is powerful in helping you laser your focus on your goals. Could you place pictures of your goals throughout your office or on the wallpaper on your phone or computer? Could you change your passwords to reflect your goals? NewCarin2022! RetireHubbyin2023!

If you take responsibility for yourself, you will develop a hunger to accomplish your dreams. - Unknown

ACTION STEPS:

- Consider your Assessment scores:
- How can you level up from where you are? (Increasing 1 point at a time is progress!)
- What is one action you can commit to take to level up your networking efforts from where you currently are?

Focus on your goals:

- What are your top five business goals for the coming year?
- What is your monthly income goal?
- What would it mean to you to accomplish it?
- What is your intention for this ____?

SECTION 1
EXPAND YOUR NETWORK

I'm looking for the people who are looking for me.
– Terilee Harrison (One of my networking mantras.)

Every workday, I spend several hours on multiple video calls with business owners from around the world. I love expanding my network. There are some people I meet, and we have a positive connection immediately and stay in the conversation; and over time we become friends, referral partners, and promoters of each other's business. There are others whom I meet, and we speak just one time. There's not a huge spark, and that's okay. Every day, I get up and begin my calls believing that "I'm looking for the people that are looking for me." It's an exciting, powerful, and positive way to get through your days and to shift how you may fear rejection or being told "no" along the way.

In the following section, I will cover how to expand your network:

- ◉ Top strategies.
- ◉ Locally by networking face-to-face.
- ◉ Nationally or globally by networking online.
- ◉ By participating in networking groups (face-to-face and/or online).
- ◉ Through publishing content on social media
- ◉ Through public speaking

As you expand your network, if you resonate with this mantra, join me in looking for the people who are looking for *you,* too.

CHAPTER 1

TOP STRATEGIES TO EXPAND YOUR NETWORK

Networking is an investment in your business. It takes time and when done correctly can yield great results for years to come.
— Diane Helbig

In these times, we are all about instant gratification in building our network as we add friends, connections, followers, and fans every single day. While growing your online following is a good thing, the business relationships you take time to build in your networking are where all the real good stuff comes from. You will not create a profitable referral relationship with a "follower" you have never spoken to.

TOP FOUR STRATEGIES TO EXPAND YOUR NETWORK:

When I look back on what I have learned over the past 15 years in the business networking industry, I identified four simple, successful strategies to help expand your network.

- Level up your "connector" skills.
- Connect and talk with a new professional every day.
- Reconnect with your network
- Focus on building relationships with your power partners.

Level up your "connector" skills.

Do you consider yourself a "connector"? A "connector" is someone who connects one business owner with another business owner so that both profit. This is you being a giver to support your networking partners.

Could you do better connect others? No matter where you are at today, the following are some ways to level up your "connector" skills. The new people you meet will always remember your giving spirit, which is key for building good business relationships.

Connect with intention

With *every single person* that you meet—face-to-face or online—ask yourself, "How can I help this person?" Follow through and connect them to someone or a resource that can help them move forward in their business. "I think you should meet..." "Here is that software I told you about..."

I was reminded by Laura Neubauer of *Kaleidoscope Media Services* when you are searching in your mind for a connection for a networking partner, make sure not to focus on simply the business contacts you know, but also search your mind for personal contacts—your family, friends, co-workers, vendors, neighbors, people from church, people at the gym, people you know from your children's school or activities. Your brain works like Facebook's algorithm, and you won't see everything unless you search for it. You never know where your next golden referral will come from. Now, THIS is networking with intention and a way to level up your connector skills.

Share what you learn with others

In your journey as a business owner, you are always learning. Be willing to share what you learn with everyone you meet. It may make a huge difference for someone and greatly reduce their learning curve. They will remember you forever!

Connectors love introducing the people they meet to their networking partners. I've met some business owners who view it as drudgery to have to invite a guest to visit their networking group. If you feel that way, shift your thinking! It is a gift to introduce someone new to your network. It is a gift for this person to meet your awesome networking partners and a gift for those in your network to meet this new person. You never know who will make a profitable connection that can make a huge difference in someone's business—and it all starts with an invitation.

Connectors live by the motto "We rise by lifting others." The more you give, the more it will all come back to you.

Make it a goal to connect and begin building a relationship with at least one new professional every business day of the year.

Imagine if you connected with and talked briefly with one new professional and did this Monday-Friday for 50 weeks every year? You just expanded your network by 250+ new people! This is so doable, and it can yield profitable results.

Your goal is to meet quality professionals to refer to your clients. No matter what you do as a business owner, it is good to have a team of professionals who you know, like, and trust to refer your clients to. There will be many times your clients will ask you, "Who do you know?" If you already have already built your network and developed referral relationships, your clients will appreciate you for your recommendations. Likewise, as you refer others, they will be encouraged to refer you as well.

Perhaps you are a financial advisor, and you would like to build a referral relationship with a highly recommended tax accountant. Maybe you are a realtor, and you need an experienced mortgage professional to refer your clients to for pre-qualification. You could be an event planner who needs an extraordinary florist to refer your clients to.

Now, where will you find these new professionals to meet? By attending networking meetings. Let the event organizer know you are looking to meet these specific business owners. They would be happy to introduce you. Ask the business owners you meet at the event who they know.

Positively contribute to online groups

As you add value to online groups, it builds your credibility for their referrals to you. You can also post in the group and let the members know who you are looking to meet. (But make sure you follow the rules of the group regarding what you post.)

Ask for introductions/recommendations on your social media

This ask can generate numerous responses. Strategically create a post and make your ask. Be specific about who you are looking to meet: A digital marketer who wants to grow their business now? A credit repair professional they have done business with and highly recommend? An image consultant from Chicago or a money mindset coach from Southern California?

Once you receive the recommendation, reach out to the friend who referred you and ask if they would please "warm up" the referral for you and let the person know you will be contacting them. Be sure to follow up on the referral and thank your friend after.

Set a goal to <u>reconnect</u> with at least one person from your network every business day of the year.

Even though there seems to be a focus on new connections, never forget there is "gold" in your network. If you're like me, you have developed a vast network over the years and sometimes we forget who we know.

Start with reconnecting with some of your favorite people from the past—people you attended school with, volunteered with, worked with, went to church with, your previous neighbors, attended a training together, parents from your children's school or activities. Make a list of your top 20 and start there.

Find out what's the latest with them. Share what's been happening with you. I have found most of the time, my business owner friends are not working in the same field or they have a different focus.

Explore if there is anything you can do to help each other at this time. You will both be updated on how you can help, and—you never know -- it's possible you might be able collaborate in some way.

If there isn't a possibility of helping each other in business right now, I promise you will be happy you reached out and reconnected. It just feels good.

Focus especially on building relationships with your power partners.

One of the key concepts I teach is you should spend 80% of your time networking with Power Partners. (Power Partners are the professionals who you share clients with but your services do not compete—where it's a natural course of business to inquire about and refer services.) Some power partner examples are website designers and copywriters, skincare representatives and aestheticians, printers and promotional product companies, weight loss coaches and personal trainers.

When you network with intention and combine your goals of connecting and talking with a new professional every day and reconnecting with your network and focus on building power partner relationships, you are sure to see a great increase in the number of referrals you are receiving.

I have so much more high-level strategy to share with you about power partners. Power partners will be a key focus later in Chapters 13 and 14.

ACTION STEPS:

What steps can you take to implement these 4 strategies to expand your network?

When will you begin?

CHAPTER 2

EXPAND YOUR NETWORK LOCALLY BY NETWORKING FACE-TO-FACE

Don't adapt to the energy in the room. Influence the energy in the room. — Unknown

No doubt you have experience networking locally. (It's online networking that is newer to all of us.) If I was moving to a new area and wanted to become known and build my network in the community, this would be my plan of action. It is wise to find and join a great local Chamber of Commerce in your area, a referral group, and one other networking group that meets bi-weekly or monthly where you find your tribe. This plan can also apply to you if you are ready to level up your current participation in your community.

Find and join a great local Chamber of Commerce.

You don't have to join the Chamber where you live or where your business is located. Take the time to visit several Chambers in the area and choose to join the most active one where you believe you can get involved and create the most mutual benefit for yourself and other involved members.

Why do I tell you this? When I joined my first Chamber back in 2005, I joined the one that was in the city I lived in, and my office was located there as well. I joined without ever visiting. I just thought it was the right thing to do. The Chamber was not very active at the time, and it was very much an "Old Boys' Club".

What I didn't know was that in the next city over, their Chamber had an amazing, high-energy director. They were growing rapidly, and they had 80-100 businesspeople attending their monthly luncheons who wanted to make connections. I joined that Chamber as well.

Serious networkers join a referral group.

Referral groups are focused on, well, giving and receiving referrals. They usually meet weekly and require both a time and money commitment. However, if you're serious about wanting to create a steady stream of referrals, being part of a referral group could be for you.

Find one other networking group to be part of.

There are lots of groups out there -- women's groups, groups focused on wellness, and groups that meet once a month. While a service club like *Kiwanis* and *Rotary* is not all about networking, you will absolutely connect and build relationships with some of the most amazing business owners around. Find one other networking group where you feel you have found your tribe and commit and become active.

Here are some next steps to take to expand your network locally:

Get involved

Participate as much as you can in the groups you commit to. There is no benefit to joining groups and never attending.

Become a leader

Consider becoming an ambassador or a board member in the organizations that you join. Leaders get noticed.

Build relationships with business owners of influence in the community

Invite them for coffee or lunch. Visit their office. Sit with them at networking events.

Be active and be noticed in the community

Schedule a Ribbon Cutting event. Sponsor an event. Be supportive and attend other business owner's Ribbon Cuttings.

Volunteer

Volunteer in your community with intention. If you serve business owners, volunteering to help with vendor check-in at the popular annual community festival can connect you with businesspeople who are choosing to invest in their business at this time. You can serve and connect at the same time!

Consider getting an office in a co-working space

Co-working spaces create a synergy you cannot have at an office by yourself. You can introduce your incoming guests to the other business owners at the office, and they can do the same. You can also conveniently brainstorm ideas together.

Become a vendor at expos and community events

Most communities host events and festivals on a regular basis (like a Home Show, the Wedding Expo, etc.). If your business is business-to-customer (B2C), any community event can benefit you greatly as your target market is the attendees. If your business is business-to-business (B2B), I recommend you become a vendor at business events where the attendees are business owners. As a B2B business participating in a B2C event you can possibly sit outside for two full days for six leads. It would be far more productive for you to attend the event for a few hours and network with the vendors.

<u>Consider branding yourself as the "face" of the city</u>

This concept is exceptionally good to separate yourself from your competition. Any business owner could make this his focus, but it's an exceptional idea for realtors, loan officers, financial advisors, insurance agents, car sales professionals (and more!) I first heard of this concept in Southern California in 2012 when I met Wendell Cuffy of *State Farm* and he introduced himself as "Mr. Palmdale."

Eric Lofholm shares some excellent ideas how to expand on this concept. Maybe these ideas will resonate with you. Let's use Mr. Palmdale as an example.

What if Wendell launched an "I love Palmdale" podcast? He could interview the mayor, the owner of the Indian restaurant everyone loves, and leaders in the community.

What if he created an "I love Palmdale" Facebook Group and wrote a credibility book to share with the community and new residents to the area, *21 Things to Do in Palmdale, California.* This is a powerful concept to consider expand your network locally.

ACTION STEPS:

* What steps will you take to expand your network locally?

CHAPTER 3

EXPAND YOUR NETWORK NATIONALLY OR GLOBALLY BY NETWORKING ONLINE

The Internet is becoming the town square for the global village of tomorrow. – Bill Gates

I say, "I was networking online before it was cool." I've been introduced as, "Terilee is not an accidental online networker." Both of these statements are true!

I met James Fierce back in 2014. At the time, James could clearly see "networking in the virtual world." At that time, I had been with *TEAM Referral Network* for seven years, networking face-to-face with thousands of business owners throughout Southern California. James shared his vision for networking online with me, and I was intrigued and introduced James to *TEAM* Founder, Kelli Holmes. She immediately said, "Let's do this!" With James' vision and my experience in networking, we began laying the groundwork and started launching several online networking chapters.

We learned over the next year that both people and technology weren't quite ready for online networking. Most people (even experienced networkers) thought we were crazy. Our members and attendees were crammed in *Google Hangouts* limited to ten people or less so you could never host a large meeting or grow a networking group in a meaningful way. We put a pause on our virtual chapters after one year but moved forward firming believing that online networking was the way of the future.

I continued networking face-to-face in Southern California until my family made an international move to Singapore in June 2017. At the time, I had been actively networking in the greater Los Angeles area for over 10 years. Now I needed to learn how to navigate running my business remotely from Southeast Asia.

I quickly learned there are many aspects of running a business virtually that I loved, and I could even continue networking and making connections online.

As I began looking around at the online options, I suggested to Kelli Holmes, "I'd like to try online networking again." She readily agreed. I hosted our first online Info Meetings in October 2018. By then, *Zoom* was able to accommodate a large number of attendees. I still had a lot of small business owners telling me they preferred networking face-to-face, and they couldn't imagine networking on screen!

I continued growing our global online referral community at *TEAM Referral Network Virtual Chapters* throughout 2019 and was looking forward to more growth in 2020 when Covid-19 brought the entire networking world online in March 2020. I was sitting there waiting for you all to join me.

Sadly, James passed away a few years ago, and I'm convinced he smiles down upon us every day as we network online saying, "I knew it!"

Virtual networking is here to stay.

While online networking has been available for many years, it took the Covid-19 pandemic for many business owners to try networking on screen. It quickly became clear to all that face-to-face networking is no longer a requirement to build your network and grow your business.

Do you have a "borderless" business where you never have to meet a client face-to-face to serve them? Virtual networking can allow you to increase your impact as you build business relationships with professionals nationally and/or internationally: you no longer have to focus on building your business in your local geographic location. No commutes. You can network online from your office, home, or virtually anywhere on the go.

The scope of what you can ask for expands. Want to expand your business in Florida? Are you attending a conference in New York and want to connect with some key professionals? Just ask your networking partners for introductions.

How to Stand Out at an Online Networking Event.

Here are some top ways to be noticed when you attend a virtual meeting.

<u>Be prepared:</u>

- ◉ Have the contact info you're going to share in the chat ready to copy and paste!
- ◉ Have your commercial or pitch (including your Big ASK) ready to go.
- ◉ And grab some water (or coffee or tea!) Sometimes we go from meeting to meeting after all.

<u>Be professional:</u>

- ◉ Be professional in your appearance and with the background you display behind you.
- ◉ Stay engaged throughout the meeting.
- ◉ Mute when you are not speaking.
- ◉ Aim to leave your video on at all times!

<u>Be uninterrupted:</u>

- ◉ If you're Zooming on your computer, put away your phone and turn off notifications.
- ◉ Create a private place to network in your home or office if you can.

Be a STANDOUT participant!

- Shine when it comes to your commercial/pitch. Think BIG! Be specific.
- Participate in the chat in a positive way.
- Be an excellent note taker.
- Grab the chat.
- Make a note of the people you want to connect with. If you can, reach out to them in the chat and send them a link to connect with you.

Be ready to follow up:

- Follow up as soon as you can after the meeting. Set a goal to follow up no more than 48 hours after.

Top Strategies to Grow Your Network Online

Let's face it. This whole virtual networking world is "new" to all of us. The more you network online, the more you will see there are many opportunities available to you to grow your business nationally (and even globally!). How do you level up your results from where you are? Here are several top strategies:

Fill out all your online profiles professionally and completely.

As you know, you never get a second chance to make a first impression. What if you are active on *Facebook* and meet a potential client or referral partner there and they visit your *LinkedIn* profile, and you haven't updated it in years? Will they be impressed by what they find? So, schedule time every quarter to review and update your online profiles. Here are some tips to help you:

- ◉ <u>How do your profiles look?</u>

  Use an exceptional profile pic. Select a headshot that displays the best version of you in a professional way.

- ◉ <u>Complete the entire profile</u>

  Different platforms offer different features. Take the time to fill in all requested information completely. You will find there are professionals offering resources on each platform you may want to follow to learn some more advanced techniques.

Actively post and engage on social media

The idea is to "know others and be known." Whatever you do, be active on the platforms where your audience is. For example, business-to-business professionals spend more time on *LinkedIn* than *Instagram*.

Shauna Smith is a Branding Strategist with the *Marketing Muse 360*. She models active posting on her social media with a nice balance of positive quotes, sharing her daily activities including networking events and sharing her expertise, sharing her travels and cute grandbaby pics, and following up with a call-to-action from time-to-time about her business.

Strategies for collaborating with online networking partners are different from your face-to-face networking partners. While you may be used to getting to know new professionals you meet by grabbing a cup of coffee at your favorite local coffee house down the street, you can now fill your schedule with phone and video call appointments with your virtual networking partners from the comfort of your office, home, or on the go. (Here's the good news! You can still have coffee if you'd like.)

Because I mostly make international business calls, I use *Facebook Messenger* and *WhatsApp* for a lot of my communicating. *Zoom* is also an excellent tool for virtual calls and meetings.

Here are some out-of-the-box ways to collaborate with virtual networking partners:

- ⊙ Always be thinking, who can I connect this person to?
- ⊙ Share their social media posts.
- ⊙ Introduce them to your friends/connections through livestreaming.
- ⊙ You can co-host a speed networking event together online. You can both invite your friends and introduce your people to each other.
- ⊙ You can co-host a webinar together.
- ⊙ Invite your networking partner to be a guest on your podcast.
- ⊙ You can introduce your networking partner to a potential client via conference call or on a video call.
- ⊙ You could "team up" to host an online five-day challenge together that highlights both your expertise.
- ⊙ Could you collaborate and host a Virtual Summit?
  The possibilities are endless!

Join online groups to expand your network.

Joining and participating in groups on *Facebook* and *LinkedIn* is an excellent way to connect with like-minded professionals from around the world.

- ⊙ <u>Finding groups on *Facebook*.</u>

  It's easy to find groups in your niche on *Facebook*. Simply go to the search bar and type the category of group you are seeking to connect with, such as entrepreneurs, podcasts, or social media. A list will pop up and you can click on "see all". Review the name of the groups that appear, read their brief descriptions, and notice how many people are already in each group.

26

⊙ <u>Finding groups on *LinkedIn.*</u>

You can see what groups you are part in the left-hand column by scrolling down on the home screen on *LinkedIn.* You can further click "see all" to see all groups you have joined. To gain access to view other groups you may wish to join, click "search other trusted communities that share and support your goals."

A word about participating in online groups to expand your network.

It might be tempting to join the biggest groups in your niche. Why not make the most connections possible, right? But keep in mind that bigger is not necessarily better. Some groups will have rules and guidelines you must follow in order to participate and stay in the group. The more guidelines the group has, the less you will be spammed and the more content and true connections you may find. It may be better to participate regularly in a couple groups than to be part of many groups and never participate at all. After you see which groups you resonate with the most, become active. You may want to volunteer to be an Admin, you may post tips regular basis to add value to all, or you may choose to be a sponsor of the group to keep your business in the most visible position possible. The most important thing, just like networking offline, is to take the time to build relationships.

<u>Some final tips on online groups:</u>

Make it a daily part of your routine to spend 'a bit of time' in a favorite group or two. For example, set your alarm every day at 2 pm to spend 20 minutes posting/engaging with other group members.

Make regular targeted posts looking for introductions, "I am looking to meet this type of business." Follow up with those who reply. Continue to build the relationship with those people who are a good fit for you.

You may also be ready to start/host your own free online group to add value and "stay in the conversation" with those you meet.

Now that you know more about expanding your network through participating in online groups, here are some strategies for expanding your network nationally and globally.

Top strategies for expanding your network nationally/globally.

From that fateful meeting with James Fierce in 2014, I was always able to see the opportunity to network nationally across the US. What came as a delightful surprise to me was that professionals would want to expand their business to other countries, and that I would be able to help them. Business owners from North America want to expand to the UK (and vice versa). Canadians want to connect the US (and vice versa). South Africans want to connect with North America and the UK. Australians want to expand to the US (and vice versa).UK professionals would want to connect with Australians (and vice versa).

What I've learned about global networking.

I've had so many conversations with professionals over the last few years. I would say, "You are my first friend from (name of country). Would you be willing to answer some questions for me about what the business climate is like there?" I have always found people are happy to help! (I'm embarrassed to say, but sometimes I would ask this question while searching online for where their country was located!)

One of the biggest issues with expanding your business globally is the disparity amongst currency rates. Having an exploratory conversation with your new business friend about the pricing of your goods and services and how that would generally be received in their country is a foundational place to start. I have always felt in the business networking industry that paying for an annual membership and for members to invest in themselves was a good thing. We appreciate things more when we have some "skin in the game." But it's not supposed to be designed to be painful. There are some countries that when my pricing translates, the cost of a networking membership is one month's salary. That's not going to work for them, and clearly some adjustments need to be made if you are going to expand in that country.

There are some countries like South Africa or India where the professionals there can do super well connecting with North Americans. But the question is how can they reciprocate in giving referrals? It's absolutely something to consider as you continue to expand.

You know I believe in the idea, "It's not what you know. It's who you know!" As a "borderless" business owner, I have found that expanding into another country can more easily be accomplished through the relationships you build. Start with one conversation at a time and see where things lead. You will know when it's right to move forward.

Top recommendations for working across multiple time zones.

I grew up in a small town in Ohio, and I never would have imagined that one day I would be working with business owners from around the world and have a global working schedule. Who knew one day I would live in Singapore and accommodate business owners from North America, Australia, the UK and many more countries!

I have always loved the flexibility that working for myself provides. Some people would look at my calendar these days and say, "That's not for me!" Not everyone would want to wake up and begin working right away in the morning, and some days have meetings at bedtime and beyond (with breaks in between). But I have found a way to make it work.

I have six strategies to share with you for navigating working across multiple time zones as you grow a global business:

1. <u>If you can, ease into working across multiple time zones.</u>

   Add in 1-2 time zones at a time. You don't need to be "all things to all people" when you are just starting out expanding globally.

2. <u>It's pertinent that you take into consideration your family/ those you live with.</u>

   Your "crazy" multi-timezone work schedule will absolutely effect them—setting alarms in the middle of the night, staying up late, getting up super early, etc.

   Having the support of your family is so meaningful as you grow your business. I let my husband, Terry, know, "I'm working tonight." That's his cue I will be staying up late or setting an alarm to take a nap and wake up to attend a meeting. I appreciate his encouragement to do whatever I need to do to grow my business.

3. <u>It's okay to ask if the people you are working with can accommodate your schedule.</u>

   Perhaps you can still speak at a summit but be one of the last speaking slots of the event so you can get up early in the morning instead of setting an alarm in the middle of the night. Maybe the podcast recording you are looking to book can be scheduled a time that is more friendly for you. It's all about the ask.

4. <u>Self-care is an absolute must.</u>

   When you experience interrupted sleep, it eventually catches up with you. Naps are your friend. Set a time in your calendar to rest the day of the event and again on the day after. When you care for your body, you can have the health to grow your business and reach your goals.

5. <u>Delegate when you can.</u>

You don't have to be a control freak and do everything yourself. (Really, you don't!) You can raise up leaders in your company and allow them to grow and shine. (And this will allow you to get the rest you need to keep growing your business.) You know if you are a morning person or a night owl.

6. <u>Set boundaries.</u>

It's okay not to accept every single "middle of the night" speaking engagement or podcast interview that you are asked to make. I have chosen to miss sleep no more than two times a month. That's what works for me. You might set a boundary for more or less.

I am so excited about the opportunities that abound for all who wish to expand their network nationally and globally. If you are ready to level up your global growth or to get started, I recommend you begin networking online with professionals in the country you want to expand in and explore where things go from there.

ACTION STEPS:

✢ What steps will you take to expand your network regionally, nationally or globally?

CHAPTER 4

GETTING THE MOST OUT OF NETWORKING GROUPS (FACE-TO-FACE AND/OR ONLINE)

Surround yourself only with people who force you to level up.
— Unknown

The truth of the matter is you never need to join any networking organization to be successful. You can attend free events forever if you'd like. But there are many networking organizations that offer some fantastic benefits to help you grow your business. (So, I say "Why not join?") I've always found it's more productive to network with others who invest in themselves.

There are many types of networking organizations out there, (local Chambers, referral groups, and women's groups are a few) and now you have more options than ever on how you network: local/face-to-face, online, and hybrid.

So, how do you know which organization is best for you? Ask yourself:

1. Do you feel like you've found your tribe?
2. Are their offerings what you are looking for?

Now is a good time to assess what organizations you are part of and to ask yourself what new organizations you would like to visit. Keep in mind, you should belong to at least three different organizations.

As you do the assessment, remember networking and building relationships takes time. While you can get a return on your time and investment sooner, sometimes it can take 6-12 months on average to begin receiving referrals. Be willing to be a giver and invest the time. I promise you will reap the rewards!

Commit to a few groups, but don't overcommit to the point that you cannot attend their networking meetings regularly. Consistently show up and remember that building relationships is the key to networking with intention!

If you're considering leaving an organization, I invite you to give it one last go, and play full out for 60 days. Maybe there is something you missed! Consider 60 days playing it full out with what you learn here about *High Level Networking.*

Consider what is your "tipping point"?

The tipping point in networking is from the time you first meet someone to the time they first begin referring you. Some professions have a short tipping point. For example, let's say you meet someone in wellness, and you're looking for exactly what they offer and ready to buy today. It happens! Some professions who have a longer tipping point are realtors, loan officers, or financial advisors—positions with a high trust factor. Because of that high trust factor, it can take 9-18 months to build trust with your referral partners and to receive your first referral. But once you do, they will continue coming in.

So before bailing on your group, try giving them those 60 more days. Because of the investment you have already made in building your network with a particular group, you may just be at the cusp of getting to the results you are looking for. Patience is important!

And one other thing before you bail. You may also want to contact your leader/head of the organization and chat about what you can do to get more out of it.

ACTION STEPS:

* List all the networking organizations you are currently a member of.

1. _____

2. _____

3. _____

4. _____

5. _____

* Consider: How long have you been a member? Have you been active? Consistent? Playing all out? Are you satisfied with the results from your networking efforts? Circle the top 1-2 organizations you intend on staying with.
* Name five networking organizations you were a member of in the past.

1. _____

2. _____

3. _____

4. _____

5. _____

* Circle any organization you would consider visiting again. (Lots of things have changed--things may have changed for you and things may have changed for them.)
* Name up to five networking organizations (new to you) that you would like to visit.

1. _____

2. _____

3. _____

4. _____

5. _____

❧ Circle the top one or two organizations you will visit first.
❧ Take action: Research when the organizations you want to visit are meeting next, block off the time in the calendar to visit, and then follow up with those you meet.

CHAPTER 5

EXPAND YOUR NETWORK THROUGH PUBLISHING CONTENT ON SOCIAL MEDIA

Before LinkedIn and other social networks, in the sales world,
'ABC' stood for 'Always Be Closing.' Now, it means 'Always Be
Connecting.' – Jill Rowley

In the past, you would most likely meet someone face to face, and then find them online and connect with them. More and more, people may find you online first!

It's critical that you spend most of your time on social media where your clients are. Depending on what you do, your clients may hang out more on *Facebook* or *Instagram* or *LinkedIn*.

In your social media, it's important that you show evidence of walking the walk, not just talking the talk. What do I mean by that? If I am a networking expert, I should have posts of me hosting networking meetings, speaking about networking, attending networking events, etc. If you are a health coach, there should be posts of you eating right, drinking water, and exercising (not eating lots of burgers and fries with a huge chocolate shake.)

Here are three types of posts that help your clients and prospects bond with you/learn about what you do:

1. **Stories**

   Here are some stories you could you share (written content with a picture or even a short video): How you helped your clients.

About your clients. A business lesson you learned. A funny story that happened recently. The story behind your company (or product) name. Something you struggled with in your business.

Most importantly, when sharing a story, be unique and authentically you.

2. Social Proof

It is important that you share testimonials. You can share a screen shot and say:

I just love waking up in the morning and seeing this!

This really made my day.

This why I love what I do.

You can also ask ambassadors to share your info as a third-party endorsement.

3. Call to Action

Every once in a while, share exactly how to do business with you. Here's a pattern you can follow: *Give value, value, value. Ask.* For example, *Join my program here. Visit my group here. Sign up for my free workshop here.*

Here are some social media post ideas to get you started:

- Share a business tip.
- Share your workspace.
- Your business mantra.
- Share your business anniversary.
- Throwback of you at your business.
- Announce a new product.
- Shoutout a mentor or hero.
- Share your morning routine.
- Share your favorite resources (apps).
- Post where you'll be speaking/making appearances.

- Share a charity you've partnered with.
- Post about something on your bucket list.
- Ask your audience how you met them.

I hope this list helps you!

Regarding *LinkedIn*

Because you are most likely a business owner, I want to invite you to take a look at how you are showing up on *LinkedIn*. It's "the place" to be for business owners who are looking to grow their network and connect with success-minded professionals from around the world.

I had a profile on *LinkedIn* for *years*, but I didn't realize until the beginning of 2020 there was a thriving culture for entrepreneurs to network on the platform. I mistakenly thought it was designed for "corporate" professionals, found it to be boring and that you were to only connect with people you already know. I would stop by once or twice a week, post a quote, not engage anyone and head back over to *Facebook*.

Then one day with just a couple new connections, my *LinkedIn* feed began to change, and I realized how wrong I had been! I wish I would have known sooner, but it's never too late to begin to build your network on *LinkedIn*. I would never attend a networking event and only talk to people I already know, so why would I network on *LinkedIn* in the same manner? It's taken some intention, but over the last year or so, I have grown from 1,800 to 23,000 connections and counting.

Whether you are new to *LinkedIn* or a veteran on the platform, here are some top tips to help you get the most out of it as your build your business network:

Ask to connect with business owners you would like to meet.

While it would be easy to reach out to EVERYONE you meet on *LinkedIn*, no one has time for that! Focusing on the professionals who share your clients first will allow you to be more efficient with your networking time.

Never be tied to making a sale. Be all about the relationship.

There are plenty of professionals on *LinkedIn* who may show up in your messaging who don't quite get this yet. However, you don't have to be one of them! When you make a new connection, always strive to get to know the person better. Set up a time to chat, learn more about what they do and explore ways you may be able to help each other. It's these relationships you grow that you take the effort to grow that can make all the difference in the world for your business (and theirs, too.)

Be memorable. Stand out from the crowd (in a good way!)

Be yourself. Share your story. Tell stories of how you help your clients. Laugh at yourself. Make and share videos. Allow your connections to get to know you for who you really are. If there is something that makes you unique, share it. I say, "I have a Super Girl cape, and I'm not afraid to wear it." You never know when my Super Girl cape will appear in a *LinkedIn* post! What is it that makes *you* memorable?

Ask for what you need.

It's okay on *LinkedIn* to share a "call to action." I make a point of sharing content daily and giving all along the way. But every so often, you can share an "ask." What is it you need in your business that would make a huge difference for you at this time? Here are several examples of asks:

- My company is looking to expand in Australia. Who do you know?

- I like to be connected to others who do what I do. Who do you know who runs a business networking organization anywhere in the world?
- I need help getting more followers on *YouTube*. Do you know someone that could help me?

When others connect to you online, they can get to know you better through the:

- LIVEs you broadcast/are a guest on.
- Quotes/posts you share.
- Articles you write.
- Podcasts you host/or participate on as a guest.
- E-book you offer.
- Credibility book you write.

If you're ready to begin producing and sharing more content, I invite you to visit the *High Level Networking Vault* and access the *How to Become the Most Published Expert in Your Industry* e-book by Eric Lofholm and me. This how-to book will guide you every step of the way how to stand out among the crowd.

ACTION STEPS:

- Which social platforms will you focus on at this time?
- What social media posting strategies will you implement?

CHAPTER 6

EXPAND YOUR NETWORK THROUGH PUBLIC SPEAKING

Public speaking skills are an essential key to achieving career advancement and success. – Robert Moment

Public speaking can be a huge part of your marketing strategy. There are so many opportunities to speak at face-to-face events and workshops, at virtual summits and gatherings, and on podcasts, livestreams and in *Clubhouse* rooms.

If you plan on speaking regularly, creating a Signature Speech, a Speaker Info File for event hosts, and writing a Speaker Introduction will help you immensely.

Create a Signature Speech.

There is value in creating a signature speech that allows you to be ready to speak at all times.

What information should you include in your signature speech?

Focus on sharing your ability and educating others about what you do.

- Who are you looking to meet?
- Share how you transform lives by sharing benefits not just the features.

Consider sharing your top tips and strategies.

Here is a sample signature speech so you can see what I mean. Some of this content may seem familiar to you! I gave this speech both pre-Covid when online networking was new and not widely accepted and after the arrival of Covid when everyone had to try networking online because it was the only networking being offered in the world. It is still relevant today:

Top Strategies for Growing Your Business Network in the Virtual World

1. Five points:
   a. Know others and be known on social media.
   b. Make new connections online daily.
   c. Reconnect to your network.
   d. Take part in online groups.
   e. How to promote your network online.
2. Expand on and share #1.
3. Expand on and share #2.
4. Expand on and share #3.
5. Expand on and share #4.
6. Expand on and share #5.

By creating your signature speech and having a *PowerPoint* presentation ready to go, if someone asks you to speak for 15 minutes, 30 minutes or an hour, you can be prepared. If someone asks you to share your Top Three Tips, you choose three.

Here are some suggestions to consider whenever you present:

- Invite happy clients to attend to support you.
- Thank your networking partners for the referrals given to you in the past.

- Paint the picture with photos, props, and visual aids.
- Ask questions of your audience to get them to participate.
- Ask for any final questions (allow a minute or two for Q&A).
- Close with a call to action.

Whenever you speak, allow time to include:

- What is your Big ASK? Who is a good Power Partner for you?
- Testimonials.
- Always offer some type of giveaway/prize. A way to stay in the conversation with you.
- Share how to connect with you.
- Offer a lead magnet (a checklist or e-book) or an opportunity to coach with you.

Create a Speaker Information File.

Save yourself time and create a Speaker Info file on Google Drive to share with event and podcast/livestream hosts every time you are booked to speak.

What to include:

- Your short bio. 2-3 sentences about who you are and what you do.
- A longer bio. (Several paragraphs).
- Several favorite headshots.
- Offer 2-3 presentations you like to give: Include the Title and several "You will learn"/Top Takeaway points.

Once you create the speaker information file once, it's easy for your assistant to share it as needed.

Create an effective speaker introduction.

Create an effective speaker intro and share it with your event host every time you speak. It will help you establish credibility with your audience by starting out right!

Here are some things an effective speaker introduction should include.

- Be brief. Aim for about 1-3 minutes at the most.
- Include your name and how to pronounce it. (Rhymes with...)
- Your title and Company name.
- What do you do in one sentence?
- Where are you from?
- Include a little-known fact, a special talent, relationship or community service. (Sometimes I add in "Terilee has a Supergirl cape and is not afraid to wear it!")

The goal is to make your speaker introduction short, informative, and interesting!

ACTION STEPS:

- Create your sharable speaker info file.
- Write your speaker introduction.
- Develop your signature speech.

SECTION 2
BUILD REFERRAL RELATIONSHIPS

There is "plenty" for everyone.
– Terilee Harrison (One of my networking mantras.)

Some businesses use cold calling as a primary way of prospecting. Because I have been business networking for so long, I have always spent my time focusing on building referral relationships. Over the years, there have been seasons when business came easy and others when it seemed more challenging. Considering what you focus on expands, no matter the season, when you approach building referral relationships with the belief there is "plenty" for everyone, that is exactly what you will attract.

In this section, I will cover:

- How to build referral relationships:
- How to show up powerfully when you network.
- How to create a winning business commercial blueprint.
- How to get revolutionary results with the "Big ASK" growth system.
- The importance of "doing your work" in high level networking.
- Implementing top 1-to-1 session strategies.
- An exciting effective presentations game plan.
- Your story matters to your networking partners.

If you resonate with this mantra, I invite you to embrace it, too, as you build referral relationships.

CHAPTER 7

HOW TO SHOW UP POWERFULLY WHEN YOU NETWORK

*Be confident. Too many days are wasted comparing ourselves to
others and wishing to be something we aren't. Everybody has their
own strengths and weaknesses, and it is only when you accept
everything you are and aren't that you will truly succeed.*
— Unknown

The Importance Of "Doing Your Work" In High Level Networking

You know you want more results from your networking efforts.
You've got BIG goals. Your have your WHY. You know the
important things you want to accomplish. To get what you want, you
have to ask for it, and having the confidence to ask for what you need is
a HUGE deal.

Let's get real. Are you showing up powerfully in your networking
to help you reach your BIG goals? If not, it's time to shift your thinking.

It is crucial that you "do your work" and build belief in yourself and
know your worth if you want to consistently attract the right power
partners and referrals. In this chapter, I address overcoming shame,
building confidence, and strategies for introverts to help them network
more powerfully.

I haven't always shown up powerfully when I network. In fact, I
spent many years barely stepping out or taking big action that would help

me more forward in my business. I didn't play full out. In fact, I played small. You see, I spent many years not believing in myself:

- I was an excellent quitter.
- I didn't think I knew enough. I always thought I needed to sign up for another training.
- I majorly fell down on my follow up.
- I didn't think I deserved to make good money.

I have learned most people worry they are not good enough and it can hold them back from who they are meant to be. Do you know what I mean? Have you been there?

We all experience shame and no one talks about it. Shame is when you feel bad about yourself as a person. (Guilt is when you've done a bad thing.)

Shame comes from three places:

- Physical/emotional abuse you may have experienced.
- The things you have done you're not proud of.
- Awkward feelings about how you are made.

I will briefly address these three places:

<u>Physical/emotional abuse you have experienced.</u>

Did you know over one-third of everyone walking the planet has been abused in some way? Many times, people hold their experience in secret and never tell anyone. What you stuff down deep inside will eventually come out in some way—addiction, depression, self-sabotage and so on.

<u>The things you have done you're not proud of.</u>

We've all done things we are not proud of. No one is exempt. We are not made to be perfect. We will make mistakes. We will err in judgment.

You may hang onto something you have done and want to keep it secret because you fear what other people will think of you.

<u>Awkward feelings about how you are made.</u>

These awkward feelings are personal. What can cause you intense shame could be no big deal to someone else. It doesn't mean you are wrong to feel bad about yourself. It just is what it is. You can believe you're too fat, too thin, too tall, too short, your skin is too dark or too light, you have a scar somewhere prominent, you have too many freckles, you are dyslexic and have trouble reading. The list is endless.

We all have a story. Every story is different. Every story matters. This is mine:

For years, in my business and networking activities, I worried people wouldn't want to do business with me if they knew the *real* me. So, I held back. I didn't create meaningful, authentic relationships. I would reach some level of success, and then I would self-sabotage.

This all stems back to my childhood. No one abused me when I was growing up. In fact, I had one of the most loving supportive families ever. But I beat myself up every day believing I wasn't good enough and it wasn't okay to be me.

I had several health challenges starting from the time I was four, and by the time I was 14, I had three major surgeries. There was one issue that affected me the most emotionally.

Puberty is an awkward time for EVERYONE, but for me, it was absolutely brutal. I was born with a rare condition where my reproductive system is underdeveloped. I needed to have surgery to begin menstruating as a 12-year-old girl. Back in the late 70's, the way it was presented to me, I took on that I was different than ALL other girls.

Let *that* sink in for a moment.

While I looked okay on the outside, I was crushed and debilitated on the inside. And for 30 years, I overcompensated by pursuing perfectionism, I felt unlovable, so I looked for love in all the wrong places, and while I did well in school and in my career, I always found a way to ruin the good things in my life. Deep down, I didn't like myself and didn't believe in myself, and my life was usually messy.

What changed for me? I left the corporate world and began working for myself. That's when I was exposed to personal and professional development for the first time. In a conversation with a coach friend one day, he asked about my childhood. I thought, "He thinks I was abused!" I said, "I had a great childhood", and upon reflection added, "but I was sick a lot". He got me thinking, and that night I went to my computer and searched for some of my symptoms of having an underdeveloped reproductive tract. No one was more surprised than me to discover that I wasn't the only one with this issue. (We didn't have the Internet back in the late 70's to access such information, and I had stuffed this all deep down inside.)

I have a condition one in 5,000 women have and no one talks about it. We are born with underdeveloped reproductive tracts, kidney abnormalities, and skeletal issues like Scoliosis (the reasons for my other two surgeries.)

Learning I wasn't alone helped me bust through a lot of the baggage I had carried for so long. I further discovered women with MRKH don't find out they have it when they are 12 and ready to start their period. They find out later in their teens when they haven't started it yet. Then they learn they have no uterus, and they will never have children.

I was blown away by the fact I had birthed two children of my own, and this is quite unheard of in the MRKH community. I thought I was junk for so many years, and I had been a miracle the whole time and had no idea! I let go of more of my baggage. I was and continue to be so grateful to God for making me a miracle—even though it seemed for so long that I I it was not okay to be me.

In the years since, I have absolutely done my work and continue to do so. I love myself, believe in myself, and am able to grow and do more things than I ever thought possible. It's because of doing my work that I

49

am able to share this book and my 15 years of networking experience with you today.

One of the most powerful lessons I've learned in my life is *one of the greatest gifts you can give yourself is to allow others to love you for who you really are.*

You may know exactly what I mean, and you have "done your work" to let go of your past. Or you may be realizing you've never addressed an issue (or multiple issues).

Doing your work is one of the best investments you will ever make in yourself. Talk to a counselor. A coach. A mentor. Your minister. Work with a hypnotherapist. There is no need to let your past hold you back for even another day.

I invite you to experience freedom. Self-belief. Self-acceptance. Value your worth. Happiness. Joy. Growth. Success.

When you are free to be you, you will show up more powerfully in your life, for your family, in your business, and as a networker.

And then there's the lack of self-confidence.

Another issue that can get in the way of showing up powerfully in your networking is having a lack of self-confidence.

Do you feel confident when you attend networking meetings? How about when you follow up with a business owner to explore how you might be able to refer each other?

Self-confidence is the trust or faith you have in yourself and your abilities. (Don't confuse self-confidence and self-esteem. Self-esteem is the opinion you have of yourself.)

Did you know:

- ◉ Your feelings of confidence and positive self-esteem affect how you think and act, how you feel about others, and how successful you are in life.

◉ Just because you are self-confident doesn't mean that you can do everything.

◉ Even when you make a mistake, if you're self-confident, you continue to be positive and to accept yourself.

◉ If you are a self-confident person, typically you don't fear challenges, you are able to stand up for what you believe, and you have the courage to admit your limitations.

We all have areas in our lives where we feel competent, yet we know there are areas where we don't feel confident at all. Is there an area you are not confident in that you know affects your networking? If you could conquer this, it would produce major results in your business!

Ask yourself: What would it mean to you to become confident in this area? What can you do now to help you be more competent in this area?

This reminds me of when I first began networking and had to speak publicly. As you know, speaking is a part of networking activities. I must confess. I haven't always felt confident as a speaker. I remember a time years ago when I had to participate in a speaking exercise at a training I attended. Each participant had to draw a subject from a jar to talk on two minutes (with only one minute to prepare). I drew a subject I had very little knowledge on, I wasn't confident in my speaking abilities, and I fell apart. I barely spoke for 30 seconds and stood there the rest of the time shaking and crying.

Here are some ways to become more confident:

◉ Set realistic goals. As you reach them, step-by-step you will develop confidence.

◉ Practice and enhance your skills.

◉ Emphasize your strengths. Focus on what you know you can do instead of what you can't.

It's been years since that dreaded speaking exercise when I failed miserably. Soon after that incident, I joined Toastmasters, and I have been speaking ever since. I now speak on big stages, host regular livestreams, teach on webinars--you name it. Most people would never know how much I once struggled as a speaker. You CAN become more confident in the things you don't feel good at.

Here's another powerful concept I have learned: If there's something you would like to accomplish or try, it can be easy to think, "I'll do it when I feel ready."

Know that you'll <u>never</u> be ready. That feeling is <u>never</u> going to come. Step up and out and do the thing that scares you. You will gain confidence, and you will be glad you did.

> *It's a terrible thing, I think, in life to wait until you're ready. I have this feeling now that actually no one is ever ready to do anything. There is almost no such thing as ready. There is only now. And you may as well do it now. Generally speaking, now is as good a time as any.* — Hugh Laurie

Have you ever lost confidence in your ability to network because of a past challenging networking experience?

It's important that you understand your feelings so you can work through it. When you lack self-confidence, it's not necessarily because you lack ability. You just may be focusing too much on someone else's unrealistic expectations--or even your own. If you are newer in business, the last thing you want to do is compare yourself to your competitor who has been in business for 20+ years.

Challenges to your self-esteem and confidence are a part of everyday life. The important thing is to learn how to overcome failure and negative experiences. This will take time and energy, but the good news is self-confidence and self-esteem are learned, not inherited. A lack of confidence does not have to be permanent.

How do you become a more confident networker? One of the best ways to grow your confidence is through doing. Network as often as you can. You will never know your limits unless you push them!

<u>"But I'm an introvert!"</u>

Now that you are developing your confidence muscle, I want to speak to all the introverts out there who feel networking is difficult for them.

Introverts can show up powerfully when they network, too!

Being an introvert doesn't mean you're shy. It means you tend to focus more on internal thoughts, feelings, or moods rather than seeking out external stimulation.

Introverts tend to enjoy spending time with 1-2 people instead of large crowds.

Networking events can feel challenging to an introvert. They can feel overwhelmed, and afterwards, they may need time to recharge. Introverts recharge by themselves, while extroverts recharge by being talkative and social.

That being said, you CAN become a "trained" introvert. In fact, I am a "trained" introvert. I have learned to love networking, but I may feel drained after attending a large event. And that's okay!

Here are some top ideas to navigate a networking event as an introvert:

<u>Network with a friend.</u>

I have always loved going to face to face events with a friend. We would act as each other's "wing man." We might separate and meet some people and then come back together when I could edify my friend, and say, "Have you met Suzanne? She is an amazing photographer!"

An introvert can work the room with a friend and focus on the friend while meeting other people. Hopefully this can reduce your overwhelm.

Be prepared.

When you go to an event, know what you want to share with the people you'll meet. Will you be asking them to join your book launch team or be inviting them to attend a workshop? When you're prepared, you can reduce feelings of overwhelm.

When "working the room," stay at the edge of the space.

You use less energy along the edge of the room talking to a person or two than when you go into the middle of all the people.

Know your limits.

If you know you can handle an hour in a crowd at a time, it's okay to leave an event early or arrive late. Set yourself up for success.

Allow time to recharge.

I have learned to allow time after attending an event so I can recharge. Self-care is so important! I like to recharge in the quiet, and even sometimes lay down for 30 minutes.

This has been a HUGE discussion.

But it's critical to your success to take the time to address shame, lack of confidence, and how to work around being introverted when you network. I have to ask, have you invested in yourself? We are all good at investing in our business but taking time to work on you is vital. Personal growth and development are a lifetime journey. It's like peeling back the layers of an onion. Once you deal with the big stuff, over time you can work on the other stuff that comes up. If you want to show up more powerfully when you network, I recommend you start within!

ACTION STEPS:

- What steps can you take to "do your work"?
- What are new things you tried in business that you learned you could do?
- What actions can you take today to become more confident in your networking?

CHAPTER 8

HOW TO CREATE A WINNING BUSINESS COMMERCIAL BLUEPRINT

Many a small thing has been made large by the right kind of advertising. – Mark Twain

I wasn't born a "Super Networker."

The truth is my first networking meeting was a bust.

I'm certain I made a terrible impression that day. You see, near the start of the meeting the host smiled and looked me in the eye and asked, "Teri, would you tell us about yourself?"

(Remember, this was my first meeting.) She did not announce it was time for one minute business commercials, and even if she had I wouldn't have known what that meant.

She asked me to share about myself. So, I sat there and told everyone *all* about me—what business I was in, where I was from, that I was married with two kids. I went on and on. I'm not sure how long they let me talk.

After I finished, all the other attendees stood up and gave a polished one-minute business commercial complete with a fancy tagline that rhymed. I felt *so* stupid.

I had no idea in that moment that in the future I would be an expert helping thousands of business owners to perfect their pitch. When I find there is someone new to networking on screen or in the room at a networking event, I always do all I can to help them feel more confident and "in the know."

In this chapter and the next, I am going to share with you my winning two-part formula for creating a powerful one-minute business commercial that gets results.

A word on business commercials.

Crafting and delivering an on-point business commercial and sharing it with your referral partners on a regular basis can be one of the most powerful, productive ways to grow your business.

Keep in mind, at some networking meetings, you may only be allowed 30 (or even 15) seconds to deliver an intro. You want to be prepared no matter what to share who you are and what you do with clarity.

Getting clear on your message is important, as one of the biggest mistakes business owners make in their networking is assuming the people you meet understand what it is you do. You might meet them once. You might run into them once a month. You might see them weekly. But what do they understand about what you do?

How do you know? Ask your business friends (the ones close enough to you to be honest!) if they understand your pitch clearly. The goal is for those who are hearing your commercial to say, "I know how to help him/her!" Or "I think I need your services."

What is a Business Commercial Blueprint?

Your Business Commercial Blueprint is a strategic outline that describes who you are and what you do. When you craft it with intention, it helps business owners you meet to understand who you are, what you do, and what you are looking for. Your concise messaging attracts them to want to reach out to you.

Let me ask you, how many times have you heard a fellow networker ramble on and on about a bunch of stuff you don't want to know and they "lost you" in the confusion? By creating a Business Commercial Blueprint, I guarantee this won't happen to you!

The simpler the language in your blueprint, the better. You will lose the people you are meeting. There is no need to try and impress them with "expert" language. It catches them off guard. They begin thinking, "I don't know what that is."

The goal of the blueprint is to be clear and concise and save 20-30 seconds inside every single one minute commercial you give to share what you are looking for.

Here's a BUSINESS COMMERCIAL BLUEPRINT template:

Give your name and company name.

What do you do (in one sentence)? *I ACTION VERB my TARGET MARKET with* _____.

Where are you located? And where do you serve clients? Or where would you like to expand your business geographically?

What is your " Big ASK"? (We develop this further in Chapter 9.)

And include "And a good power partner for me is a _____." (See Chapter 13).

Close with your motto, creed, or tagline.

Let's break this five-step Business Commercial Blueprint down:

Step 1. *Give your name and company name (or name and title if you are your brand)*

Could this be any easier? You've got this step!

As an example, I say, "I'm Terilee Harrison, and I'm a Networking Strategist and Coach.

Step 2. *What do you do (in one sentence)?*

You can pack a lot of "punch" in one sentence. Here's what I mean:

I ACTION VERB my TARGET MARKET with _____. (HOW DO YOU HELP?)

Here's mine as an example: I help coaches, consultants and solopreneurs network in the most dynamic and lucrative way.

Do you already describe your business in one sentence? Are you happy with it? If not, use this time to level it up. If this is new to you, let's do this!

Here are some sample action verbs. Choose the one that resonates most with you:

- ◉ help
- ◉ supply
- ◉ support
- ◉ provide
- ◉ encourage
- ◉ assist
- ◉ teach
- ◉ serve
- ◉ boost
- ◉ promote
- ◉ train

Here are some sample target markets:

- business owners
- women
- men
- parents
- seniors
- families
- children
- corporate professionals

Speaking of target markets, it's possible you may have not narrowed down your niche yet (or you are looking to change your focus). To create a steady stream of referrals, it's imperative that you share with your networking partners what ideal clients you are looking for. Think of it this way—your business friends are busy sharing their own business commercials. They don't have time to think about how to help you. But, if you ask for what you are looking for in a specific way, they may be able to assist!

If you say you can work with somebody, anybody, and everybody, it will get you nobody as a referral.

Who are your ideal clients? Write down your favorite clients who you like working with (now and in the past). And who is your dream client you would love to serve? Include it in the list.

Here's an example of some of the top professions who do well in my global online referral organization: Business coaches (Start up, Branding, Book, Productivity, Success Coaches—there's all types!), Life Coaches, Virtual Assistants, Web Designers, Digital Marketers, Social Media Experts, Financial Advisors, Bookkeepers, Health & Wellness Professionals, Sales Experts and more.

Note: Your "how do you help" should be concise, but catchy. It's great if it causes people to say, "Tell me more."

As you talk about what you do, be sure to keep it "simple." Sometimes I think business owners feel the need to sound like an expert, but you need to speak to your audience in a way they can understand you or they won't understand what you do. This can cause them not to want to connect with you. It reminds me of Kim Jacques with *Lifewave*. Kim and I were leveling up her commercial, and she said, "I can speak in 'Jedi' and tell all the science behind my products, but I know I should speak in 'non-Jedi' so the people I'm connecting with can understand.

When you have invested the time to nail down what you do in one sentence, you will begin to attract your ideal clients and the help you are looking for from your networking partners. This will lead to more of the referrals you are looking for!

And I have good news! As a bonus, you can use this one powerful sentence in many ways in your networking. It's the answer to "What do you do? anytime you're asked. It can become part of your social media bios and headlines. It can be a key part of your speaker introduction. And more!

Step 3. *Where are you located?*

> *And where do you serve clients (or where would you like to expand your business geographically)?*

When you share your location, it paints a picture for your networking partners. We begin to ask who do I know in that area? And when you get specific about where you serve clients, we expand the search in our mind:

- ◉ My market is in Southern California including Los Angeles, San Diego and the Inland Empire.
- ◉ I serve clients from the UK and South Africa.
- ◉ I am ready to expand my business in Australia.
- ◉ I am looking to meet referral partners in Dubai.

Here's my example: *I am located in Singapore and serve professionals throughout the English-speaking world.*

Over the years, I have heard so many business owners say, I work with clients "anywhere." And I just don't think it's true. If you will get specific about what you're looking for, your networking partners will absolutely help you. I once knew a business owner who worked for a Sheriff's Department in Southern California and did plumbing on the side Mondays, Tuesdays, and Wednesdays only within 30 minutes of their city. Because he was super specific, those were exactly the referrals he received. Ask for what you need, and your network will deliver!

Step 4. *What is your " Big ASK"? (We develop this further in Chapter 9.)*

Include "And a good power partner for me is a _____." (See Chapter 13.)

Step 5. *Close with your motto, creed, or tagline.*

Other professionals who are meeting you for the first time and hearing your commercial will "lose" your name and company as you share it. It is a great idea to close out with sharing your name, company name, and motto, creed, or tagline if you have one.

If you are part of a larger company that has paid a lot of money to create a tagline, use it! Or you can always create your own. Your tagline should be clever and attention getting. I've heard realtors say, "I don't sell houses, I sell homes." Skincare people have used, "If your skin isn't becoming to you, you should be coming to me."

If you network regularly with a group of referral partners, they know you and your business well and can be a good resource to help you brainstorm a new tagline.

Next, you will create your own Five-Step Business Commercial Blueprint. Access your Blueprint worksheet in the *High Level Networking Vault.*

Your BUSINESS COMMERCIAL BLUEPRINT template:

Give your name and company name.

What do you do (in one sentence)? *I ACTION VERB my TARGET MARKET with* _____.

Where are you located? And where do you serve clients? Or where would you like to expand your business geographically?

What is your " Big ASK"? (We develop this further in Chapter 9.)

Include "And a good power partner for me is a _____." (See Chapter 13).

Close with your motto, creed, or tagline.

Some final thoughts on your business commercial:

Write your commercial out on paper or type it and save it on your phone. Read it! You don't have to hide behind the paper or have your head down in your phone—make eye contact and smile whether you're on *Zoom* or networking in person). I'd rather you read your commercial than wing it. You will forget something. Over time, you will memorize your Business Commercial Blueprint, and then you can put your paper or phone away!

Practice reading your commercial with a timer. Make sure you allow plenty of time to include your Big ASK.

Get feedback from a trusted networking friend or two. Ask your friends, "Do you understand my message clearly?" Make any adjustments necessary.

In the next Chapter, you will develop 12 Big ASKs to include in your commercial to help you get the referrals you are looking for and to reach your goals even faster!

ACTION STEPS:

* Write your commercial out.
* Read your new commercial at your upcoming networking meetings.
* How does it feel?
* Are you getting better results?

CHAPTER 9

HOW TO ACHIEVE REVOLUTIONARY RESULTS WITH THE "BIG ASK" GROWTH SYSTEM

When you've figured out what you want to ask for, do it with certainty, boldness, and confidence. – Jack Canfield

Mastering the art of making Big ASKS when you network is serious business, but I do have a funny story I must share. The first time I networked on screen with Australians (with my Midwest US accent), I was given the opportunity to share a few networking tips. One of the tips was, "You have to put your Big ASK out there when you network." After I finished sharing, I muted myself and took a breath thinking, "Well, that went okay!" The host went onto the next item on the agenda, and I glanced over at the chat which was quite busy. I saw: *Are we allowed to swear in this meeting?* And I thought, My goodness! Someone is swearing in the chat. I couldn't help myself—I began to scroll up the chat to see who was swearing and why. I basically lost track of networking meeting going on. I would have never guessed. They thought it was ME! She (and a few others) didn't hear the 'K' when I said, "Big ASK".

Online networking lesson learned: be careful to enunciate very clearly when speaking online (and especially when networking with business owners from other countries where your accent may be less familiar.)

Back to serious business. To create a steady stream of referrals, it's imperative you share with your networking partners the ideal clients you are looking for. Think of it this way—your business friends are busy sharing their own business commercials. They don't have time to think about how to help you. But, if you ask for what you are looking for in a specific way, they may be able to assist!

Let's start with a challenge to all referral partners everywhere.

True confessions. I've been a member of several business referral networking chapters off and on since 2006. Looking back over the years, I can honestly say I could have been a better referral partner. I could have been more specific about what I was looking for to help them refer to me. There were many times I wondered why I didn't receive more and better referrals, but I never took the time to look in the mirror. I just thought they weren't great givers. I didn't realize I needed to show up differently to make it easier for them to refer to me!

Now, I would never say you should be "selfish" in your networking. The best networkers focus on being the best referral giver possible, yet I think it's important to pause and embrace the fact: to get what you want, you must ASK for it.

I'd like to ask you now:

- What are your BIG goals for your business?
- Why is reaching these BIG goals important to you?
- Are you happy with the results you are receiving from your networking efforts?
- What referrals have you been asking for?
- Have you been taking this opportunity seriously as a way to help you reach your BIG goals?
- Do you think if you communicated what you need in a bigger, more specific way, it would help increase the quality and quantity of the referrals you are receiving?

I want the time you invest in referral networking to be extremely valuable to you and the meetings you attend to be not only fun, but highly productive and effective for all. (I think that's what we all want!) The

66

challenge is that you must help your networking partners as they strive to give you good referrals by delivering a BIG, specific "Ask" each week in your one-minute business commercial.

What do I mean by that?

A "Big ASK" is… Sharing what you seek next for your business in a clear, specific way. This goes beyond asking for an introduction to one client at a time! Think BIG. It's okay to be audacious in your ask such as: "I want to connect with Oprah!" If your referral partners chuckle at your request, you're on the right track!

Focus on your ideal clients. You might say, "Business coaches are a great referral for me."

How can you ask for an introduction to more than one client at a time? "I would like an introduction to people who train business coaches."

Consider asking to meet your competition. Do your services complement each other? Could you collaborate with them? As an example, I would say, "I like to meet other professionals who run business networks from around the world."

Who are your power partners? In addition to your Big ASK, always include, "And a good power partner for me is a _____."

What a Big ASK is not:

- ◉ "Please LIKE my *Facebook* page."
- ◉ "Please attend my upcoming workshop."
- ◉ "I would like to get together with you one-on-one for a one-to-one session."

Those are okay asks, but if you have HUGE goals, the referrals you will receive from these asks won't help you reach them anytime soon. If you only ever ask for others to LIKE your *Facebook* page (or the equivalent each week), it makes it challenging for your referral partners to give you good referrals. Believe me, they know you, like you, trust you, and want to help you! You can help them better refer you by asking for what you need in a way they can hear it.

How can you make this happen? Stop winging it! Don't wait until you're arriving at or logging on to your next networking meeting to decide what you will ask for. Be thinking about your next Big ASK all week long. If you start focusing on sharing a Big ASK in your networking, you will find you will start to receive more referrals and introductions. You get what you focus on.

<u>Let's get real.</u>

I invite you to rate yourself on a scale from 1 to 10. Have you been winging it? Or are you nailing your Big ASKs?

A "1" would be, "I haven't been trying very hard." A "10" would be, "I totally get what you're saying, and I'm asking BIG!"

Truthfully examine how you are showing up and ask yourself what you can do to increase your impact. Even if you check in at a "7" or above, ask yourself how you can level up your ASKs to help get you more of the results you are looking for.

Your BIG goals matter! You matter. Let's do all we can to cheer each other on and help each other GROW.

A great first step is you've got to make your commercial "sticky".

I have an Italian networking friend who taught me how he makes spaghetti. He shared that to be able to tell when the pasta is cooked through, you should pull out a single piece of pasta from the boiling water on the stove and throw it against the wall to see if it sticks. If it sticks, it's done!

Just like your pasta sticks to the wall, you want your commercial to be sticky. Inside your business commercial, when you share a specific request to your networking partners—like you're looking for speaking engagements or you need a connection to a publisher, you turn on their reticular activators. The Reticular Activating System (RAS) is a bundle of nerves at our brainstem that filters out unnecessary information, so the important stuff gets through. The RAS is the reason you learn a new word and then start hearing it everywhere. Or when you buy a new car and you never saw that car or maybe that color before and now, they are everywhere!

When you share a specific ASK with us, our brains will get to work searching to see if we can help you. Every networking meeting I attend, I write down what the attendees ask for and refer back to the list to see if I can make a connection and help them on the spot. So many times, there is a blank by the names of the attendees who don't make an ask. Now that you know the "science" behind this, don't let that be you ever again!

If you're not getting what you want from your networking group, I invite you to look in the mirror. What have you been asking your networking partners for? Today is the day you can change your ASK and change the results you are getting.

It's important to ask, are you ready to receive what you are asking for?

Having confidence in your ASK is crucial. I have understood Big ASKS for years, and from the time I first launched virtual networking chapters in Fall 2018, I began asking to connect with "on fire" health and wellness leaders with "on fire" teams who want to share networking training and online networking opportunities with their people.

Sounds good, right? When I first began asking for this referral, I had maybe two online chapters (we were just starting out!) and as I made the request, inside there was a part of me that thought, *What would I do with the people if I actually got this referral? I have no place to put them!* With this kind of mindset, how many of these connections do you think I initially made? You're right. In the beginning I didn't. But over time as I built the network and became more confident that I could serve more people; these ASKS have become referrals and relationships that are leading to fruition. "Do your work" and you will experience the benefits!

Part Two of Business Commercial Blueprint.

This is one of the most powerful exercises you will do in high level networking. You will gain clarity on who your best clients are, learn how to ask to connect with more than one client at a time, get clear on how to ask to meet your competition and share which power partners you would like to connect with most.

When you are clear on what you want, you can share it with your networking partners so they can connect you. These connections can create a steady stream of referrals for you and help you reach your goals!

Who are your best clients?

Write down as many as you can of your favorite types of clients who you like working with now (and worked with in the past). And who is your dream client you would love to serve? Include it in the list. There are examples following to help guide you.

1. _____

2. _____

3. _____

4. _____

5. _____

6. _____

7. _____

8. _____

9. _____

10. _____

11. _____

12. _____

How can you ask for more than one client at a time?

Look at your list of ideal clients and ask yourself, "Who works with a lot of these types of professionals?" For example, instead of asking to meet a podcast host, could you instead ask to connect with a podcast coach who would know a ton of podcasters? Do you see the difference? Use the examples to follow to find the perfect way to level up your ask so you are asking for more client at a time every time you network.

1. _____

2. _____

3. _____

4. _____

5. _____

6. _____

7. _____

8. _____

9. _____

10. _____

11. _____

12. _____

Who is your competition?

I recommend you should always talk to your competition and get to know them. It's important to explore what each of you do and discover what niches you serve. It's possible they serve a niche you don't, and you can refer clients to them, and they can refer clients to you, too.

1. _____

2. _____

3. _____

4. _____

Who are your power partners?

Power partners are professionals who share your clients and they do not compete with you. We have discussed power partners briefly, but you may want to wait until you have read Chapter 13, How to develop power partnership relationships to create a steady stream of referrals before completing this section.

1. _____

2. _____

3. _____

4. _____

5. _____

6. _____

7. _____

8. _____

9. _____

10. _____

11. _____

12. _____

Following are some examples to help you with your brainstorming. While this is not all encompassing, be creative and explore where your business fits within these categories. For example, let's say you are in the travel industry. Do you prefer to refer back and forth with business owners or do you focus on retreats and work with wellness professionals as a niche? The following examples are for "business and marketing," "real estate and finance," and "beauty and wellness."

Business & Marketing –

Who are your best clients?

- Business coaches (Start up, Branding, Book, Productivity, Success Coaches—there's all types!)
- Life coaches
- Virtual assistant
- Financial advisors
- Bookkeepers
- Beauty & wellness
- Social media experts
- Website designers
- Sales experts
- LegalShield
- Mailbox Power/Send Out Cards

How can you ask for more than one client at a time?

- In person speaking events. Online speaking opportunities/Virtual Summits.
- Podcasts and/or Livestreams
- Teach in Facebook Groups
- Leaders of Direct Sales/Network Marketing Companies
- Trainers of my clients

Who are your competitors?

- Who are other people who do what you do?

Who are your power partners?

- Podcast coaches
- Digital marketers
- Business coaches
- Sales trainers
- Printing/promo products
- Book coaches

Real Estate & Finance

Who are your best clients?

- People in transition:
- Graduated/new job
- Newly married
- Married and having children
- Divorced
- Laid off
- Relocating for work
- Retirement
- Death in family

How can you ask for more than one client at a time?

- In person speaking events. Online speaking opportunities/Virtual Summits.
- Podcasts and/or Livestreams
- Lunch & learns for companies
- Workshops/webinars with power partners
- Newsletter swapping

Who are your competitors?

- Other people who do what you do.

Who are your power partners?

- CPA
- Estate planning attorney
- Financial Advisor
- Real Estate/Mortgage
- P&C Insurance
- Banker
- Senior care
- LegalShield
- Pre-Need Planning
- Money Mindset Coach
- Credit Repair
- Life/Business Coach
- Contractors
- Solar

Wellness/Beauty

Who are my best clients?

- Couples.
- Professional women.
- Speakers.
- Busy Moms.

- Children.
- Entrepreneurs.
- Those experiencing low energy
- Those experiencing anxiety
- Those ready to lose weight
- Those ready to get in shape
- Ready for change

How can you ask for more than one client at a time?

- In person speaking events.
- Online speaking opportunities/Virtual Summits.
- Podcasts and/or Livestreams
- Teach in Facebook Groups
- Leaders of Direct Sales/Networking Marketing
- Trainers of my clients

Who are your competitors?

- Who are other people who do what you do?

Who are your power partners?

- Skincare
- Functional Medicine
- Personal Trainer
- Hypnosis
- Reiki
- Weight Loss
- Life coach
- Relationship Coach
- Nutritionist

To network at a high level with intention:

Set a monthly appointment yourself—possibly the first Monday of the month. Review your monthly goals for your business. Select 4-5 Big ASKs to help you reach these goals (one for each week.) The reason for this is that you want to vary your ASK regularly. Your networking partners are looking for you to give them something to work with. When you ask for the same referral request several weeks in a row, it's easy for your networking partners to think, "I didn't have anybody for you before, I don't have anyone for you now." And they may stop looking to help you until such time as you ask for something new.

Success tip.

It's important to share what is the best referral you've ever received. You never know, your power partners might be able to replicate it (or come close!)

Okay, so, you get it that you need to make BIG ASKs to help you get increased results from your networking efforts. But now what?

Here are nine strategies to help you expand your confidence as you ASK (BIG!) for what you need to help you reach your goals:

1. Let your faith overcome your fear. One of the main reasons many people do not get what they want is they are too afraid to ASK. Some people fear success. Some fear failure. Some fear they aren't good enough to serve their Big ASK. Know that you will never feel ready, so don't wait on that feeling to come. Focus on having faith in your abilities and strengths and ASK anyway.

2. Believe you will receive. You need a solid level of certainty and expectation when you ASK for something you want. Focus on how it will feel when you sign on your dream client; how it will increase your bank balance; and how it will get you closer to your goals.

3. Think before you ASK. Make your ASK a top priority when you network. Be certain what you will ASK for before you click the button to join any online meeting. Always be prepared.

4. Sell yourself first, then you can sell others. When you're confident in fulfilling your ask, that's when you will be able to sell others. Step into your greatness.

5. Make your ASK clear and specific. Write out exactly what you want. Then revise until your ASK is clear. Practice! Talk through your ASK with networking friends, close colleagues (or both!) to be sure it makes sense.

6. Keep your WHY in mind. Every time you make your Big ASK, let your networking partners see your heart. All our WHYs are so important. When they understand your WHY, they will want to help you more!

7. What's in it for them? When you're ASKing, always be sure to explain what's in it for the person they will refer and how they will benefit and win.

8. ASK as many times as necessary. And in as many places as necessary (networking events, one-to-one sessions, on social media, with your power partners). Your tenaciousness and perseverance will undoubtedly pay off.

9. Remember to say, "Thank you." Honor the referrals you are given as the "gold" they are and more will be given to you.

Now that you have developed some Big ASKs, I invite you to get comfortable sharing them with other business owners. Your network wants to help you. You only have to ask them for what you need! Now let's explore some top strategies for effective one-to-one sessions.

"BIG ASK" BRAINSTORM ACTION STEPS:

- Who are your ideal clients?
- Who are your competitors?
- How can you ask for more than one client at a time?
- Who are your power partners?
- List as many asks as you can.

CHAPTER 10

HOW TO IMPLEMENT TOP ONE-TO-ONE SESSION STRATEGIES

What makes networking work is that it sets up win win situations
in which all parties involved get to take something home.
Networking is a sharing process. Until you understand that, you
won't have much of a network. — Earl G. Grave, Sr.

When I first began networking, I didn't get it that "networking" on its own doesn't work, but "building business relationships" does. I mistakenly thought I needed to be a member of multiple Chambers of Commerce plus other networking organizations. I spent a lot of time (and money!) attending networking events thinking I needed to be "known" by many to make connections. I did little connecting in-between meetings, so while many professionals knew of me and my organization, I didn't know many of the people I had met in a real and meaningful way. I didn't get relationship marketing.

Let me ask you, what do you think I got out of these networking efforts? Not much. And, looking back, I find it sad, because I was meeting lots of professionals at the time and if I would have tried at all, I could have given my fellow networking partners many referrals as well.

One of the best ways to build a relationship after you meet a new professional (at a networking meeting, the Chamber, through a referral, or anywhere!) is to meet with them one-on-one to get to know them better and explore how you can help each other.

You can do a one-to-one session virtually, over coffee (my favorite!), at one of your offices, before or after a networking meeting, or even over the phone during drive time.

What a One-to-One Session is not:

A One-to-One Session IS NOT where you ask to meet with someone and spend the entire time telling them what you do and trying to convert them into a client. This portrays an attitude of "how can I sell this person."

Think of it this way: Have you ever been networking, and someone backed you into a corner and it was clear they weren't going to let you out until you bought from them? It feels slimy, right? If you only talk about yourself and don't show interest in the other person during a one-to-one session, it's slimy times 10. I'm certain that's not how you want to be remembered.

Coach to Collaborate.

A One-to-One Session should never be all about you. Check your level of reciprocity. You want to go into the appointment focusing on "how can I help this person?"

Take turns asking and answering the following sets of questions.

About business:

- What do you do?
- Share your marketing materials.
- Who is your ideal client?
- Who are your power partners (the professionals who share your clients and they don't compete with you?

Personal:

- What is your background?
- What other organizations do you belong to?
- Share about your personal interests. For example: Coffee or NFL football.

Moving forward:

- How can you help?
- Who can you connect them to?
- What resources can you provide?
- Are there any ways we work together?
- What are our next steps?

If the appointment has gone well, set another time to chat.

Focus on laying a foundation for understanding how to bring referrals to each other in the future. Be willing to give first. Giving is the best way to elevate your level of reciprocity.

Uh oh. I didn't know.

What if you didn't know how to do a One-to-one Session and you focused mainly on yourself? Reach out to the person and ask to meet with them again. You could say, "We really didn't get to talk about what you do when we got together. I would love to learn how I can help you."

It's never too late to elevate your level of reciprocity!

Here are some top tips for booking One-to-one appointments.

Use an online scheduling link like www.calendly.com. Decide how much time you want to allot per appointment. This is typically 15, 30, or 60 minutes.

To save yourself time, ask strategic questions through your booking system. (Here's a sample of what I ask.)

- How long have you been in business?
- What type of business are you in?
- What current challenge are you facing in your business?
- What is your income growth goal?
- Who is a good power partner for you?

Don't be afraid to create your own questions that are right for you!

Strategize your availability. Are you available daily or specific days each week? Set boundaries. Allow time for working on your business. Create openings in your calendar that are right for you.

Create a One-to-One Session Profile.

You can further optimize your time by pulling together your information once in PDF form and sharing it at all your One-to-one sessions.

Some networking organizations offer online directories as part of your membership. As an example, at *Virtual TEAM* our members can optimize their Member Profile at TEAMreferralnetwork.com. The SEO built into the website can help you be found online.

I took the same information in my One-to-One Session Profile and included it in this online directory. Now I have two ways to share my information—either online or by sharing the PDF.

Check out what online directories you have access to through the networking organizations you are part of. Perhaps you can do the same!

Note: All the info to create my One-to-One Session Profile had already been created. It came from my *LinkedIn* profile, my speaker introduction, and my Big ASK and Power Partners Brainstorm. I hope yours could be easy to create, too!

Here's what information you may want to include:

- Name/business name
- What I do
- How I create value
- Who I'm looking for/possible power partners?
- What to tell others about me
- Contact info
- Skills
- Interests

- Experience
- Groups

To see a sample of my One-to-One Session Profile, visit the *High Level Networking Vault*.

ACTION STEPS:

- Set a goal. How many one-to-one sessions do you want to hold each week? (Remember to prioritize one-to-ones with your power partners first.)
- Complete your One-to-One Session Profile.

CHAPTER 11

HOW TO DEVELOP AN EFFECTIVE PRESENTATIONS GAME PLAN

If you don't go after what you want, you'll never have it. If you don't ask, the answer is always no. If you don't step forward, you'll always be in the same place. — Unknown

Many networking organizations you are part of may offer the opportunity to be a featured speaker. To make the most of this opportunity, you must emphasize sharing what you do and what help you need in your business at this time.

Since I began working in the business networking industry in 2006, I've heard thousands of small business owners' business presentations. One has always stood out to me. One of my *TEAM Referral Network* members from California worked for *Wells Fargo Commercial Loans*. I remember when I first met her and learned her minimum loan was $2 million. I had originally thought I might not be able to easily refer her. I was visiting her chapter meeting one morning when it was her turn to speak.

She arrived with one of those large three-fold cardboard stands students use for their science fair projects. Do you know what I mean? She included: These are some of the clients I like to do business with. These are great power partners for me. These are the types of businesses that are excellent referral sources for me and more!

After that effective 10-minute presentation, I felt empowered to be able to help her and make connections for her! We should all strive to be that effective in our presentations, and with your Big ASK and Power Partner Brainstorms, you can be.

Over the years, I've seen it all when it comes to speaking presentations. I have seen a hairstylist curling a woman's hair, a mechanic demonstrating how to repair a carburetor, and a coffee shop owner show us how to make a waffle. While these demonstrations were all highly informative, and I learned that these business owners had expertise in their field, I didn't learn in detail how I could help to bring them referrals.

When it's your turn to be the featured speaker, remember this is your chance to share with your networking partners what you need! Take advantage of every second of this opportunity. Don't spend this time showing how you do what you do. Tell them what help you need to grow your business. They are there to help and are waiting for you to share this information. Remember to paint a picture for your networking partners: Tell stories about how you have helped clients. Share the benefits of working with you. Always think BIG and be specific about your needs.

In addition to your networking partners, who else should you tell what you need? Everyone! But specifically, share at any networking meetings you attend, on social media, tell your clients, referral partners, and your family and friends.

The following are excellent ideas to share in your presentations to educate your networking partners about what you do. Take notes of which areas stand out to you that you want to cover next time you speak.

What is a good referral for you?

Always be sure to share what is a good referral for you. Throughout the following sections, I'll use my company, *Virtual TEAM*, as an example. Maybe it will spark something you can share about your business! Good referrals for *VTEAM* are:

- ⦿ Invite guests to visit a weekly chapter meeting or online event.
- ⦿ Share us on *Facebook* and *LinkedIn*. Invite business friends to our *Facebook Group*.
- ⦿ Invite me to meet your people, even for 10 minutes at a weekly meeting.

At *VTEAM*, we are looking to connect with small business owners. New businesses are good, but mature businesses are always better. We like to connect to non-profits who serve families and children. And we want to meet the professionals you know who you see as an excellent networker.

Who are your ideal clients?

Share who you like to work with. At *VTEAM*, we work with life coaches, business coaches, website designers, virtual assistants, sales trainers, social media experts, book coaches, insurance professionals, accountants, IT people, and more. But we can help any borderless business grow their business through referrals.

What professions would you like to build business relationships with?

At *VTEAM*, we like to build relationships with companies who train coaches and "on fire" leaders of "on fire" teams—whether health and wellness, *LegalShield* or a beauty company. Who do *you* like to build business relationships with?

Who are your best power partners?

At *VTEAM*, we power partner with others who work with small business owners, like heads of other networking groups, and businesses who help their clients market their business, such as printing companies and website developers.

Is there anything new in your business you want them to know?

Share the latest about what's happening with your business. *VTEAM* offers "Community Membership". You don't have to belong to a weekly chapter meeting to be part of our global online referral community. This is perfect for people who just cannot fit a weekly meeting into their schedule.

Where are places you would like to speak?

If you tell us where you would like to speak, we can make key introductions for you. At *VTEAM*, we like to speak on podcasts, livestreams, at virtual summits, to *Facebook Groups* who serve our audience of small business owners, to network marketing team meetings/webinars, weekly sales meetings at companies, and so on.

What topics do you speak on?

Share your favorite speaking topics so we can match you up properly to an organization's needs. For example, I can speak generically on relationship marketing and networking or customize a presentation for how a specific business can grow through referrals.

Are you looking to hire people?

What positions do you currently have available? At *VTEAM*, I am building a team of global ambassadors and am looking to meet connected people who love networking and helping others.

Are you looking to expand?

Share with us the geographical area you are wanting to grow your business in. At *VTEAM*, we want to continue to expand throughout the US, Canada, Australia, and the UK. We are open to expanding elsewhere as well.

Do you offer any incentive programs?

What incentives do you offer your customers? At *VTEAM*, we offer member referral rewards: For each new member you bring into the organization, you earn a credit of one month off toward your annual membership renewal. When you consistently bring in one member a month, you never have to pay for membership again.

Are you excited now about the next time you get to speak to your networking partners? When you ask for what you need in a way they can hear it, they will absolutely help you!

ACTION STEPS:

- ❖ When is the next time you are speaking? Begin to prepare now.
- ❖ Review previous presentations you have given. If you are considering delivering the content again, ask yourself if you need to level it up in some way.

CHAPTER 12

YOUR STORY MATTERS TO YOUR NETWORKING PARTNERS

A common mistake entrepreneurs make is they don't embrace storytelling in their business. Consumers want to know the person that is behind the business. – Andrew Griffiths

I believe everyone has a story, method, or cause that the world needs to hear. When you share your story, it will help build credibility with your networking partners, and it is always encouraging to learn how far someone has come in their personal or business life. Do you know the inspiration others find in your strength to overcome challenges? Or the realization that we all have had to endure pain and suffering? There is significance of your struggles!

The extraordinary thing about sharing your story is you don't know how much others need to hear it and the impact it can have on their life. And, today, more than ever before, it's easy to share your message with others. Sharing your story can go beyond just telling your networking partners at a face-to-face meeting. We all have an amazing tool at our fingertips to help us reach the masses—our smart devices.

Your message might be telling your story of starting over after a brutal divorce. Sharing the latest strategies on how businesspeople can save more money on their taxes. (We all need that!) Or spreading the word about your foundation that raises awareness and funds for families with disabled children.

Are you ready for a personal question? On a scale of 1 to 10, where would you rate yourself in getting your message out to the world?

The 10s are crushing it. They are writing books, hosting regular livestreams, and recording and sharing videos across various social media platforms.

The 5s are saying, "I know, I know... I need to share my message." They might be taking some action.

The 1s are shaking in their boots asking, "Terilee, what are you talking about? No one would want to hear what I have to say! Who am I to be the one to give this message?"

No matter where you are on the scale of 1 to 10, I get where you are because I've been there myself. For years, I didn't share my story because I was afraid if people knew the real me, they wouldn't like me or want to do business with me.

What holds you back from sharing your message? I can tell you exactly what it is. It's the "P" word: procrastination. Procrastination can cause you to shut down and hold back from moving forward because of fear.

What might you be afraid of?

1. You fear being exposed.
   You don't share your message because you fear "What will people think of me?" To share the light of your story out in the world, you must first shed light on whatever is dark inside of you.
   Over the years as I have shared who I really am, I have learned that people want to be real. They crave the ability to be transparent. When you are real, you give them permission to do the same. When I'm real about who I am and where I've been, I've only found people embrace, love, and accept me more.

2. You fear exposing a "sticky mess."
   You may also procrastinate because some of the personal issues you would share—integral parts of your story—involve other people. You have a concern about calling out other people for things they've done or their role in a particular issue.

Let me put your mind at ease. There are things you can do to get around this in your sharing:

- ◉ You don't need to tell every single detail. There are ways to not give specific details but to get your message across.
- ◉ You can also share your story and change their names and include a disclaimer that "some names have been changed."

3. You fear that your story is not "good enough."

Believe me when I say, you are never going to feel good enough to tell your story. You will NEVER feel ready. Don't wait for that feeling to come!

But I will tell you *when* it will feel right. The first time someone approaches you and looks you straight in the eye and says, "Thank you so much for sharing your story (or recording that video or publishing that article). I needed to hear this because ..." It is these moments when you know it's the right thing to do.

I hope you will consider sharing your story, method, or cause with your networking partners. I know you will be glad you did!

ACTION STEPS:

- ✦ What story do you feel called to share?
- ✦ How would you feel most comfortable sharing it? In writing? Speaking? Creating a video?
- ✦ When will you take action and share your story?

SECTION 3

COLLABORATE WITH POWER PARTNERS AND JOINT VENTURE PARTNERS

Let's cheer each other on and help each other grow!
– Terilee Harrison (One of my networking mantras.)

Collaborating with power partners and joint venture partners will help you evolve and grow as a business owner both personally and professionally. It's the ultimate way to cheer each other on and help each other grow.

In this section, I will cover:

- ◉ How to collaborate with power partners and joint venture partners
- ◉ How to develop power partnership relationships to create a steady stream of referrals.
- ◉ How to bring together a high-level power team to achieve more profits.
- ◉ How to establish and grow joint venture partnerships.

If you resonate with this networking mantra, I invite you to incorporate it into your business culture, too.

CHAPTER 13

HOW TO DEVELOP POWER PARTNER RELATIONSHIPS TO CREATE A STEADY STREAM OF REFERRALS

Surround yourself with inspiring beings with amazing commitment to their dreams. — Unknown

Networking with power partners—professionals who share your clients and they don't compete with you—is one of the most powerful concepts in business networking. Power partner relationships take time to develop, but they can be some of the most rewarding and lucrative business relationships you will ever have. If you have the right 5-10 power partners who are actively referring you back and forth, you can have all the business that you will need. Spending 80% of your networking time building and cultivating relationships with power partners will yield you profitable results.

As powerful as this concept is, most networkers don't properly leverage partnerships and collaborations to help them grow their business. Have you ever made this common networking mistake?

Here are some facts to help understand this powerful concept:

The importance of reciprocity.

A power partner relationship should be reciprocal. You can easily refer to each other. I've heard a financial advisor share about an estate planning attorney who he had referred to for 20 years who had never given him a referral in return. This is *not* power partnering. Power partners give to each other.

Raving fans vs. power partners.

Sometimes people think a power partner is "anyone who is outgoing and talks about my business." This is actually a raving fan. Now to be clear, you want to have lots of raving fans. They are important to have, and you appreciate them! But usually, you cannot give and receive referrals with a raving fan.

Power partnering and dating.

I view meeting a potential new power partner like "dating." Depending how long you have been in your current relationship, it may have been a long time since your last first date, but I bet you still remember it. You get to know the person better. You see how you feel when you're around them. You decide whether you want to see them again. There are many times I meet a potential power partner on *Zoom*, and I can see the many possibilities of how we can work together! There are times I get so excited that I want to "marry them" on the first date.

Just like in actual dating, that's just not a good idea! It's important to take things slow and build trust and confidence in each other and learn more about each other's offerings. If you continue to feel it's a good match, you can take the relationship further and begin sharing each other's events or even perhaps co-host an event together.

Are you ready to get serious about building power partner relationships to grow your business with ease? Let me share some power partner strategies:

Who is a good power partner "match" for you?

This is a two-fold question. First, how do you know what power partner professionals are a "good match"? And second, what businesses go hand-in-hand with yours? (Go back to the Big Ask Brainstorm.) Also, ask yourself (thinking outside of the box) who can you partner with who is not a "normal" category that people would immediately think of?

Professionals in business services should seek power partners doing the same who are not their competitors. This also applies to health and wellness, people in marketing, finance and real estate professionals, too.

Also consider what "type of person" is a good power partner match for you? The best power partner match for you is when you are on a similar path.

- They've got to be "hungry"! A professional who is also in growth mode can be a good match. The person who has already reached a certain level of success may not have a need to/be interested in building power partner relationships.
- What if you're brand new in business or launching something new? Partnering with someone else who is new in business can be empowering as you share the business journey together.
- Look for the people who are looking for you. When you reach out to someone to invite them to explore getting to know each better to possibly build a referral relationship and they aren't interested, it's okay! Some people aren't going to get what you're asking. Some people are too busy. But the right people for you will reply "Yes!"

Where do you find new power partners?

Ask your networking partners and post on social media: "I am looking to connect with _____." Always seek them out first when you are networking both face-to-face and online.

How do you connect with new power partners?

Reach out and say, "I am looking to build a referral relationship with someone who does what you do to refer my clients to. Would you like schedule a time to chat and explore how we can help each other?"

How can you collaborate with your new power partners?

- Share their social media posts. (Ask them to send you specific content to share.)
- Introduce them to your friends/connections through a podcast or livestream.
- Co-host a webinar together.
- Co-create and launch a course.
- Co-host a podcast.
- Start a networking group together.
- The possibilities are endless.

A power partner case study: Meet Anne and Melissa.

Anne Ferrier Crook and Melissa Deally have been power partners for over a year. Anne lives in Nashville and is a Certified Integrative Health Coach. Melissa is from Whistler, British Columbia and is an Integrative Health Practitioner and Holistic Health Coach and Guide. One year into their business relationship (and friendship), Anne and Melissa were very excited to share with me the success they had power partnering. They wanted me to know the results they had achieved together weren't the typical "I give you a referral," "You give me a referral," but that they support each other in a variety of ways.

- First, they built their know, like, and trust factor. Anne became a client of Melissa's (at no charge) so she could experience her work. She was Melissa's ideal client suffering with gut issues. Melissa helped Anne gain her health back. This is why Anne is confident to have Melissa do her clients' lab work now—because she has experienced it herself.
- They became affiliate partners to promote each other's group programs.
- They shared opportunities to be on podcasts and livestreams and to speak at Summits. This led to an exclusive speaking opportunity which then led to 2 ideal clients signing up for Anne's monthly package.

96

- They referred valuable resources like a graphic designer, website guidance help, an opportunity to become published in a collaborative book and more!
- They introduced networking opportunities to each other, including sharing free tickets to events when possible. Many connections for speaking opportunities came through networking connections!
- Anne is now co-launching a community with three other fabulous women. Melissa introduced all of them.
- When Melissa was nominated for and earned an award, Anne was highly supportive. Melissa thanks Anne (and others!) for the votes she received.

What an amazing first year+ of power partnering! Did learning of all the connections and resources Anne and Melissa shared over the last year inspire you with ideas how you can better work with your power partners?

To increase the impact, you're making from your networking efforts, it's crucial you focus on how to level up your power partner relationships. Once you have some power partners you are actively referring, you should consider having regular Power Partner Reality Checks.

What do I mean by that? Check in with your current power partners. Review who are you currently exchanging referrals with. What can you do to level up this relationship?

Reconnect with past power partners. Is there someone you referred to in the past and, for whatever reason, you no longer refer each other? It's a good time to check in with them and learn what their latest project is and see if there is anything you can do to support them.

Repeat this process with your casual referral partners. While most of your referrals will come from power partners, repeat this process with any casual referral partners you have as well.

To get started, here is a Power Partner Reality Check where you can examine three scenarios:

1. Are you new to networking and ready to build a power partner relationship with a member(s) of your chapter? Or you are a longstanding member and new power partners have recently joined your chapter?

    Like a first date, have you had a first one-to-one session to explore who you are, what you do, and how you might be able to work together? Don't wait for someone to ask you to coach. Schedule a time to get together before you leave your next meeting.

2. What if my power partner and I have never really started referring to each other or our referral relationship has deteriorated, and referrals have dropped off?

    Like the other important relationships in your life, power partner relationships take effort and open/honest communication. Get together and ask:

    ⊚ How can I earn your trust?

    ⊚ What would it take for you to refer to me?

    ⊚ We have worked well together in the past, what has happened to change that? What needs to happen to us to begin referring again?

This is all about building a reciprocal referral relationship. Be willing to answer these questions as well!

3. Take time to evaluate long standing power partner relationships: You may have an ongoing reciprocal referral relationship with a power partner that works well for you both and is profitable. Congratulations! You still want to ask, what more could we do together to reach and help more clients?

Your "competition" can be your "greatest companion."

For several years in my business networking career, I didn't quite embrace this concept because of a negative personal experience I had with a local competitor. I had just moved to a new city in Southern California after working for my company for five years. I had started and grown many successful networking chapters. I KNEW I had what it took to start over and bring together a whole new network and serve many business owners.

To do that, I knew I had to get out and network. I decided to visit the monthly Chamber breakfast meeting. Upon my arrival, I was greeted by the Chief Ambassador with a huge, welcoming smile. She extended her hand and asked me for a "big" stack of business cards. I handed her a two-inch stack of cards and brightly announced, "I'm new in town. This is the first time I am attending a Chamber meeting here."

Everything changed when she glanced at the company name on my business cards. "I know exactly who you are!" the Chief Chamber Ambassador grimaced. "I'm the Area Director for Xxx." She worked for my company's largest competitor in the marketplace. Clearly, she was no longer glad to meet me.

Throughout the breakfast meeting, some of the business owners I met at my table kindly volunteered to me which professionals in the room were members of the Xxx networking group, implying they would not be interested in my business. I sighed to myself, "Okay..."

When the business card box was passed later in the meeting, the two-inch stack of my cards I had turned in was nowhere to be found. Wow! Someone really doesn't want me to meet new people today.

Driving into that early morning meeting that day, I hadn't been expecting such a frigid welcome. But I didn't let that stop me. Over the next five years, I built a successful referral network in that community, and while her business shrunk, mine expanded. It's a good thing I had a surplus of confidence because of my past success, and I didn't let her nasty tactics stop me that day. I would have missed a lot of amazing relationships.

Why do I share this story with you?

For a long time, because of my negative experience with this person, I thought, "Oh, they are my competition, I don't need to speak to them." Don't fall into this line of thinking.

Many times, you can come alongside your competition and be stronger and serve more clients together.

What if I don't feel qualified to "team up" with a new power partner?

"Impostor syndrome" is when you believe you are not as competent as others perceive you to be. You may feel like a phony and like you don't belong where you are. It can affect anyone no matter their degree of expertise, skill level, social status, or work background. Know that you are good enough to build successful power partner relationships with the professionals you meet.

Here are some ways to cope with these beliefs:

- Take the risk.
- Focus on what you can do (not what you can't).
- Forget about being perfect.
- Stop comparing yourself.
- Everyone has felt this at one time or another.
- You are growing and evolving.

When you focus on building power partner relationships with intention, you will see a positive shift in your business. Now we will explore how to level this concept up even further by creating a Power Team.

ACTION STEPS:

- ❧ Meet with your current power partners to discuss you can do to level up your results.
- ❧ Begin seeking out new power partner relationships. Take the time to get to know these new contacts.
- ❧ Do a Power Partner Reality Check.

CHAPTER 14

HOW TO BRING TOGETHER A HIGH-LEVEL POWER TEAM TO ACHIEVE MORE PROFITS

You need a tribe of people around you who are endlessly devoted to helping you succeed. There's power in that... — Unknown

Are you ready to elevate the referrals you are receiving from your Power Partners? Creating a "Power Team" helps you leverage your networking efforts!

A "Power Team" is group of power partners who meet regularly to review what you have accomplished so far and brainstorm next steps in how you can work together. "Power Partners" meet as a group monthly (or as often as possible) to get to know one another and to take their networking partnerships to a higher level.

Get together online (or if you're all local--for coffee, lunch, or whenever it's convenient!) Set your intention and bring your new goals to share with your Power Team members. Take notes as your networking partners share during the meeting. At the meeting, use the time effectively, so each of you can share information about yourselves and your businesses. If you are willing to bring together a Power Team and host a meeting, let your power partners know and schedule a time to meet.

When you're ready to start meeting, here is a suggested meeting agenda (make it your own!):

Power Team Meeting Agenda

- Welcome to all--especially any new Power Partners. Allow the newest Power Partners two minutes to share about their business.
- State the purpose of the meeting: Your goal is to elevate Power Partner relationships to give and receive more and better referrals.
- Progress check-in: What have we been able to accomplish together so far? How many referrals have we passed? (One person is appointed to collect this information prior to the meeting and share it with all. (Five minutes maximum.)
- What are our individual business goals for the next month? (Two minutes each.)
- Brainstorm new ways to help each Power Partner to reach their goals: Are there any possible new introductions you can make? Joint sales presentations or seminars to co-host that you could discuss? Email marketing, co-op advertising or distributing marketing materials you could do together?
- What additional "Power Partner" categories can we invite to our networking groups/introduce to each other?

Power Team Meeting – Follow up:

1. Schedule individual one-to-one sessions with newest Power Partners (if not done already).
2. Follow up with current members.
3. Schedule any meetings needed after this meeting's brainstorming.
4. Set date/location of next Power Team meeting.

Focusing on nurturing your relationships with your Power Team members will pay huge dividends over time.

If you've not developed a Power Team yet, I'm sure you find this concept intriguing! Next, let's explore another powerful way to leverage business relationships—joint ventures!

ACTION STEPS:

- ❖ Meet with your power partners and introduce the Power Team concept.
- ❖ Consider hosting/facilitating your Power Team meetings.
- ❖ Take action and begin to see the profitable results that come from high level collaboration.

CHAPTER 15

HOW TO DEVELOP AND MAXIMIZE JOINT VENTURE RELATIONSHIPS

The new form of networking is not about climbing a ladder to success; it's about collaboration, cocreation, partnerships, and long term values based relationships. – Porter Gale

Another way to leverage key business relationships is to create joint venture partners with persons of influence. A joint venture (JV) relationship could be considered a "step up" from a power partner relationship. A JV relationship is when you partner with a person of influence who believes in your product and shares it with their audience to receive a portion of the sales made. What makes it a step up? Instead of creating a steady stream of referrals, with JVs, it can be possible you will start doing the largest deals of your life.

You're ready for JVs if you've already built your email list and have already established your authority. (I will cover building your email list in the next chapter.) You should already have a product or service you are actively selling (or at a minimum a detailed idea of what you will be providing.)

Here's how JVs work

Your product, service or some other kind of resource is of interest and value to another business's audience. That business refers their audience to you, resulting in multiple new sign ups to your list (and often sales too).

An effective JV means it's a win-win for both sides. Your JV partner wins financially and by building authority with your email list. Often JVs are based on the premise of giving your partner a percentage of referred sales (for example, a 50/50 split on revenue).

Referral (or affiliate) program

You own a product and bring on as many promoters as possible. You gain new newsletter subscribers and sales made because your affiliates promote you. Your affiliates benefit through commissions made on each sale.

Podcasts

Podcasts are a form of JV, as both the interviewer and interviewee win. If you host a podcast, you get new content for your audience, grow your visibility, and build authority by associating with your guests. How about your guests? They get exposure for their own business.

Here's how hosting a podcast can grow your email list. Most interviewees will share the episode with their own audience, giving you exposure to their people as well. You will want to have a strong call to action to invite their audience to stay in the conversation with you.

Webinars

JV webinars can add hundreds (or possibly thousands) of new subscribers to your email list and can be one of the fastest ways to grow your list with no upfront cost. Unlike *Facebook* ads where you pay for ads whether they result in sales or not, you only pay commissions on products sold.

Guest posting

When you guest post, you share useful content to a JV partner's blog for a link back to your site via a bio section promoting email list growth. Likewise, when you accept guest posts on your blog, this can also help you grow your list.

Contributing content

Want to write an article inviting quotes from others in your industry? You can invite a JV partner to contribute!

This is win/win for you and all the contributors as you gain visibility and exposure when all share the content with their audiences. If you strategically include influencers with large followings, this can possibly mean a significant increase to your list.

Finding ideal JV partners.

If you know who your ideal customer is, JV partners who serve your same client and they are not competitors. The best JV partnerships bring together a natural synergy.

Who are people offering training or coaching others in your niche? You can find them online or at classes and events. You can also find them in *Facebook* or *LinkedIn* groups sharing valuable content. Look for people who are go-getters in your industry. Every potential JV partnership is unique. Some may come together quickly, and others may take a bit more time to develop. You may find yourself more successful at forming new partnerships when you share examples of how you benefited past partnerships.

What's important to JV partners.

Typically, potential JV partners are concerned about what value will be added to their audience, profitability, and how much time this partnership will take. If you're good at tech or have someone on your team to assist, you may want to consider offering to JV partners that you will handle all the tech (and capture the emails!) including:

- Build the registration and thank you page (like *Kartra* or *LeadPages*)
- Custom Sales (Promo) Page (like *Kartra* or *Leadpages*)
- Host the webinar (like *Zoom* or *GotoWebinar*)
- Host the Replay Page (like *Kartra* or *LeadPages*)

- Replay video hosting (like *YouTube* or *Vimeo*)
- Email communication (like *Mailchimp*, *Aweber* or *Keap*)
- Create graphics to share on social media (like *Canva*)

You can also provide them with:

- Pre-written email copy they can send to their subscribers
- Promotional graphics they can use to share the event information
- Pre-written social media posts they can share

Offer to let them appear as the host.

Let your JV partner know they can host the event and you will take part in the event as a guest—even if you are running all the tech in the background. This saves them time and effort and alleviates them worrying about all the event production.

Once you and your JV partner agree and set a date to work together, it's time to put your agreement in writing.

All JV's should have an agreement in writing.

All JV agreements should be fair to both parties. Put in writing what each partner will contribute and what the agreement is expected to achieve.

A written agreement should cover:

- Objectives of the partnership
- Any financial contributions by the parties
- Any assets or employees allocated
- Ownership of intellectual property created by the JV
- Responsibilities and processes
- Sharing of profits, losses and liabilities
- Resolution procedures for any possible disputes
- Proposed exit strategy.

You may also wish to sign a confidentiality agreement.

You could be ready to begin creating JV deals now, or you might need to build your email list first. Either way, building your list is a top priority for business success.

ACTION STEPS:

❧ Make a list of potential JV partners to reach out to suggesting, "I'll promote you if you promote me."
❧ Take action, reach out, and do one promotion at a time. Build your confidence muscle as a JV partner.

SECTION 4
GROW YOUR EMAIL LIST AND FOLLOW UP

Networking is "serious business".
–Terilee Harrison (One of my networking mantras.)

Networking is much more serious than most business owners take it to be. You show up every day with your "why" and your goals, purpose, and the legacy you want to leave. So does every business owner you encounter every single day. Every why, goal and purpose is *so* important. Yet so many professionals "wing it", they play small, they don't bother with an email list, they don't follow up like they should (and much more!) It's time to get over the things that hold you back and learn a new skill set if you need to so you can reach your goals even faster.

In this section, I will cover:

- How to grow your email list.
- Top ways to build your email list (even if you're starting from scratch).
- Follow up strategies to ensure high level results.

May you take all your networking—including building your email list and your follow up—very seriously and invite every networking partner you meet to do the same. Networking *is* serious business. Let's do all we can to help each other reach our goals!

CHAPTER 16

TOP WAYS TO BUILD YOUR EMAIL LIST (EVEN IF YOU'RE STARTING FROM SCRATCH)

If social media is the cocktail party, then email marketing is the "meet up for coffee." The original one to one channel.
— Erik Harbison

As I noted in the last chapter, one of the most effective, high-level ways to grow your email list is through joint venture partners. However, there are many other strategies for growing your list—especially if you are starting from scratch.

If you haven't started building your email list or your contacts are not organized, here is a story to inspire you. Eric Lofholm started building his list from scratch with no leads. He has grown his list through social media, public speaking, networking, referrals, cold calling, and joint ventures. Today, Eric's *Infusionsoft* database has 76,000+ contacts. One of the techniques he uses to promote his list is to cross-promote. He will reach out to someone like Les Brown and say, "I will promote you if you promote me."

Why is building your email list important? An engaged email list can be one of the most profitable assets in your business. It just makes everything easier. When you launch a new product, you can offer it to your list. Everything you create can bring in revenue. Growing your list can be worth thousands of dollars in sales every single year or even more. Actively growing your list with intention will be a game changer for you.

If you don't have an email list or if you don't keep your data organized, you can!

What are some of the challenges that get in the way and cause business owners to get stuck and not build their list?

- They have no idea where to start.
- They are clueless about the tech.
- They worry about what content they will share with their list.

Can you relate? Let's overcome these challenges now. To start, you should offer a lead magnet, make it easy for new subscribers to opt-in, select an email service provider, and create a weekly content plan. Then you can begin multiple list building strategies that you feel will work best for your business.

Offer a lead magnet.

A lead magnet is a valuable piece of content you offer for free in exchange for an email address. It can be as simple as a PDF guide, cheat sheet, or checklist. You can also create and offer an email course, a five-day challenge, or create a quiz and ask for an opt-in to view the results.

Ask yourself, what information could I share in a lead magnet that subscribers would say, "Wow! I cannot believe he gave this information for free!"

Make it easy for new subscribers to opt-in.

Let's talk tech for a moment. Is tech not your thing? Bring someone on your team who can assist you with helping to pull together whatever is needed to get your email list started. Ask your networking partners for a referral for this vital resource. Ask for help to make it easy for new subscribers to opt-in such as add signup forms to your website, create pop-ups and optimize landing pages.

Select an email service provider.

There are several factors in choosing your email service provider including the size of your list and whether your business is B2C or B2B. There are free email service providers available if you are just starting out. As your list grows, you can find an email service provider (ESP) to grow with you.

Create a weekly content plan.

If you want to nurture your list and engage them, it's good to email once a week. During times when you have promotions to send out, you will email more often.

What content can you email to your list? Tips and strategies, your latest podcast episode (and link), your new blog post (and link), upcoming events, and more.

You may worry about how you will keep up with creating content for a weekly email. If you follow a content calendar for all your social media, you can use the same topics for your email communication, too. An efficient way to produce content is to create a bunch of it at once.

Here are some list building strategies.

- Give a discount upon sign up, such as save 15% on your first order when you sign up.
- Create a daily deal to bring in more in-person traffic or online orders.
- Encourage your subscribers to forward your newsletter.
- Include a call to action to sign up on your receipts.
- Leverage your mobile app by including a call to action.
- Invite people to 'join the club'—possibly a birthday club or anniversary club.
- Set up a "refer a friend" program to encourage subscribers to share your list with their friends.

- Host competitions and giveaways to encourage excitement, participation, and growth.
- Create exclusivity by inviting subscribers to join for exclusive content for list members only.

Your business may be locally based, have an online focus, or could be both. Here are some ways to collect subscribers both offline and online.

Ways to collect subscribers offline.

- Ask them personally.
- Put out a sign-up sheet near your check out at your business.
- Host an in-person event and add those who RSVP online to your list.
- Business conferences and events—have a call to action/put out a sign-up sheet.
- Community festivals and street fairs—have a call to action/put out a sign-up sheet.
- Add QR codes to your business cards/flyers including a call to action.
- Networking (face-to-face)—ask the people you meet if they would like to be added to your list.
- Public speaking (in person)—have a call to action to collect business cards for a door prize to "stay in the conversation" with you.

Ways to collect subscribers online.

- Have an opt-in on your blog.
- Have an opt-in to join your online community.
- Include a call to action and opt-in links in your own email.
- Offer download freebies.
- Host an online event on Eventbrite. Eventbrite collects emails with RSVPs and also markets your event to those searching for events like yours.
- Host a webinar and collect RSVPs by email.

- Be a podcast guest and share a call to action.
- Start your own podcast and share a call to action.
- Public speaking (online)—have a call of action for a "free gift" with opt-in.

How to build your list through social media:

There are many ways to build your list through social media. Here are just a few.

- You can include a call to action to join your list in your social media bios.
- On *Facebook*, you can include a call to action on your *Facebook Cover*, ask for an email to join your *Facebook* group, and include an opt-in on your *Facebook* page.
- On *LinkedIn*, you can share a link with a call to action on your profile and in *LinkedIn* groups. You could also "feature" a post on your *LinkedIn* profile offering your lead magnet with opt-in.
- On *Instagram*, you can include a call to action in your *Linktr.ee* link in your bio and in *Instagram* stories.
- On *Twitter*, you can pin a tweet at the top of your profile.
- On *YouTube*, you can create a call to action on your videos and channel to join your list.

Which of these strategies do you think would be most effective for your business to grow your list? Which ones will you implement as you begin building your list with intention? What resources do you need to help you get started?

ACTION STEPS:

- Get real about your email list:
- How many contacts do you have today?
- Are you actively building your list?
- Are you actively nurturing your list by emailing them regularly.
- Set goals to make building your email list a priority.

CHAPTER 17

FOLLOW UP STRATEGIES TO ENSURE HIGH-LEVEL RESULTS

If you don't go after what you want, you'll never have it. If you don't ask, the answer is always no. If you don't step forward, you'll always be in the same place. — Unknown

Have you ever lost track of a contact? I'll always remember connecting with an amazing South African woman I met on *LinkedIn*. We direct messaged and said hello, and she asked if I had a moment to chat. We spoke by phone. I was so excited to meet her and looked forward to connecting with her again. And when I was ready some weeks (or a month or so) later, I could not find her information. I couldn't remember her name. I searched as best as I could on *LinkedIn*— and came back with nothing.

Have you ever made this common networking mistake? It's not one I want to replicate. Ever!

Why, oh why, don't we follow up like we should?

Sometimes you're just not ready for success (or you may fear failure).

Back in 2006, I had just written my first book, *The Business Mom Guidebook: More Life, Less Overwhelm for Mom Entrepreneurs*. I heard Carol Evans, who was the head of *Working Mother Magazine* at the time, was going to be speaking at a women's event near me. I knew she would be an amazing connection for me to reach more moms! I invested my money and purchased a ticket to the event. Fortunately, I was able to meet Carol and spoke with her. She told me, "I have been thinking we should do regular segments to reach mom entrepreneurs. Here's my personal email. Contact me." And, I never reached out to contact her!

Now, I ask myself, what would have happened if I had? I could have been nationally (or internationally!) known as an expert for mom entrepreneurs (years ago!)

By now, you know my story. I didn't believe in myself. I lacked the confidence and wasn't ready for this at the time.

Can you think of your own Carol Evans story? Have you connected with someone who would be an AMAZING, POSSIBLY life changing connection for you? How might your business and your life be different if you had connected with this person? What could you have gained? What have you missed?

Level up your mindset for follow up.

The fortune is in the follow up. I've heard this saying over and over (for years!)

Why is it you don't you do what you said you were going to do? No matter what goal you want to accomplish, you will always have your inner game competing with your outer game.

Say you want to gain ten new clients. Your "outside game" says, "I am going to sign on ten new clients in two months." But your inner game says: "You don't deserve to be successful." "You aren't a winner--you will never be disciplined enough to make that happen!" "You haven't acquired that many new clients in the last year. How do you think you can bring in that many new clients in the next two months?"

So, do you bring in ten new clients in two months? Probably not! You started skipping out on the number of calls you were going to make each day or didn't continue following up with every person who indicated they were interested because your inner game was competing with your outer game!

117

How can you overcome this? Try setting a reward or a penalty. It's got to be a reward or penalty SO big that you can't stand yourself. You've got to do EVERYTHING to accomplish your goal.

I have learned I am personally motivated by setting a penalty. I have accomplished more by setting penalties over the last four years than I had in the 10 years prior. The penalty you set has to be PAINFUL for you. Penalties are always personal. What's painful for me might not be painful for you.

Here's an example from several years ago: I didn't do my own laundry at the time. My husband did our laundry for many years. To complete a coaching certification by a certain date, I set a penalty I would do my best friend's laundry every week for four weeks (and she had a LOT of laundry!) I did EVERYTHING it took to reach that goal. There was NO WAY I was going to go to her house and do ALL her laundry for four weeks!

The next time you set a goal, remember your inner game is competing with your outer game. Ask yourself:

- How can you even out the playing field?
- What can you do differently, so you do not fall down on your follow up?
- What is a reward or penalty that you could set for your next follow up goal that would help your inner game compete with your outer game?

It's time to take control of your follow up. Let's say you have the business card of a key business connection in your hand right now. Just do it! Follow up now. Invite them to coffee or lunch if they are local. If they aren't, invite them to call you or chat via video call. Focus on the WIIFM (what's in it for me) for the person you are reaching out to.

Sometimes it's easy to make excuses and postpone making a call to an amazing contact like this because you want to be as perfect as possible. You want to impress them! But there is no need to be perfect. You are a work in progress. You will never be perfect. What's most important is that you take action!

What steps can you take to be on top of your follow up?

Here are some ideas:

Make follow up a priority.

Putting your follow up first will ensure much more positive results from your networking efforts and as leads become prospects than become closed sales. I use the "Todoist" app to help me keep better track of my follow up. It has made a huge difference for me.

Schedule time to follow up daily.

When do you think would be the best time for you to follow up each day? For some, it might be first thing in the morning. For others, it could be last thing before you finish work each day. Decide what is best for you and stick to it.

Follow up in "batches."

I learned this concept from Dan McPherson of *Leaders Must Lead*. When we met for a one-to-one, he told me, "Terilee, I will follow up with you in the next day or so. I follow up in batches." Dan will hold several meetings and then would do all his follow up for them together. I really like how following up in batches flows instead of having a meeting, following up, having a meeting, following up. If you've not tried it, see what you think!

Implement #followupfriday.

Follow up Friday is when you don't leave to "break" for the weekend until all your follow up for the week is done. This allows you to start on Monday with a clean slate.

Automate what follow up you can.

If you love tech, you probably love setting up automation in your business. If tech is not your thing, it is worth it to get the help of an expert to automate any follow up you can.

Delegate duties to a virtual assistant to free up time for the follow up you must personally do yourself. Hiring my first assistant in 2020 was a game changer for me. It frees me up to do the higher-level things I need to do.

Even if you bring on someone to help you five hours a week to start, you will see it will make a huge difference for you. You can gradually increase their hours as you grow.

Here are more expert top follow up strategies.

Change your mind set about follow up.

Colleen Strube of *Connect Develop Succeed* suggests, you can change your mindset about follow up to "I really need to love this and have fun with it." One way for you to fall in love with follow up is to implement a system and surround yourself with people who help execute it. It's easy to feel it's fun when you see the results.

Colleen also suggests, "Think of follow up like the idea of a tennis game going back and forth on the tennis court. I think of myself sometimes as an automatic tennis ball launcher that keeps shooting the tennis ball. You just you know eventually someone will hit it back to you."

Prioritizing connections.

Dhea Bartlett of *Dhea's Ideas* offers this: "I sort my connections by a '1', '2', or '3'. We are all busy and have to guard our time. It's impossible to build strong relationships with everyone you meet. I don't completely cross anyone off my list and never want to talk to them again, but it just might be months or years from now. If I meet someone who's a "1" and they really want to connect with me and I want to connect with them, I want to have the time to do that."

Sandy Zeiszler of *MoxxClicks* says, "One simple tip from online networking meetings on *Zoom* is to rename the chat to the day in the time of the events. I have one file folder in my computer for networking. All my networking activities go into the same folder. I copy and paste the information from the chat. It's actually better to copy it live instead of after you have saved it because it captures the html of the hyperlinks. Next, you can email it to yourself, because it activates all the html. I like emailing it to myself so I can go in and highlight the names that I need to follow up with. I then move them to another system to take notes when I schedule calls and conversations with these connections. All this being said, it's so easy to forget to follow up. I always say book a time 10-15 minutes after big networking events to follow through--otherwise it may never happen."

The best timing to follow up after meeting a connection.

Dhea Bartlett relates, "I read somewhere that it's important to do follow up within 24 hours. You may also know of the 72-hour rule—people will forget who you are. If I network with someone on a Friday, if I don't follow up the same day, I don't bother people on the weekend. If I don't follow up that Friday, then I definitely reach out on Monday."

Colleen Strube advises, "Even if you miss a 24-hour or 72- hour rule, you can still connect with people. Don't feel bad. They haven't connected with you yet, right? When you connect with them, you're still ahead of the game--even if it's later."

Keeping the conversation going and adding value.

Sandy Zeiszler describes her procedure this way: "When I meet a new connection on *LinkedIn*, I document it in an *Excel* spreadsheet including the date I connected. I add a second column for follow up date. When they send me a connection request (or when they accept my request), I always say thank you for connecting to start the conversation. It helps when you find something or someone you have in common to mention to keep the conversation going."

Sandy further advises, "When following up and building relationships with new connections I meet, I like to always recommend podcasts or books. When you're giving something of value, they can know that you're a trusted source."

Don't delay--Start new follow up habits today!

ACTION STEPS:

- ❧ What steps will you take to increase your follow up efforts?

SECTION 5
YOUR HIGH-LEVEL NETWORKING SUCCESS BLUEPRINT

To achieve your goals, always network with intention.
— Terilee Harrison (One of my networking mantras.)

You plan your day. You plan your goals. Yet, I bet you've never planned your networking before. Now that you will have more clarity about how to plan your networking, I invite you to include it as a regular part of your business planning process.

In this section, I will cover how to create your high-level networking success blueprint:

- How to develop and execute your high-level networking action plan each quarter.
- Your monthly network with intention check in.

Wishing you much success as you network with intention to reach your goals!

CHAPTER 18

HOW TO DEVELOP AND EXECUTE A QUARTERLY HIGH-LEVEL NETWORKING ACTION PLAN AND A MONTHLY NETWORK WITH INTENTION CHECK-IN

Sometimes the smallest step in the right direction ends up being the biggest step of your life. Tip toe if you must, but take the step.
— Unknown

By now, we have explored many ways to level up your networking. You know most networkers "wing it," and the good news is that you don't have to wing it ever again! You know that to create a steady stream of referrals, you need to network with intention.

You can pull together and package your networking plan into a Networking Success Blueprint. To access your Networking Success Blueprint, visit the *High Level Networking Vault*.

Planning out your networking strategy every quarter and checking in each month will help you create the best networking outcome possible.

Your quarterly High Level Networking Action Plan.

Set a date with yourself at the beginning of each quarter on your calendar for networking planning: January 1, April 1, July 1, and October 1.

What do you need to have with you?

- Your business goals.
- Your Big ASK and Power Partners Brainstorm.

Strategize and plan.

Review your business goals for the upcoming quarter. Are you launching a new program? Do you have sales goals you want to hit? What do you need to sell to reach these goals? Is there a contest you want to win that requires you to hit specific targets?

Refer back to your Big Ask and Power Partner Brainstorms and map out:

What will be your Big ASKs for the next 12 weeks?

What power partners you will ask to connect with for the next 12 weeks?

Link your goals to your asks.

Week	Big ASK	Power Partners
1		
2		
3		
4		
5		
6		
7		
8		
9		
10		
11		
12		

You will also link any presentations you give during this time period to your goals. What topics for presentations will you focus on during the next 12 weeks?

1. _____

2. _____

3. _____

Your monthly Network with Intention Check In.

Set a date with yourself at the beginning of each month to check in: January 1, February 1, March 1, April 1, May 1, June 1, July 1, August 1, September 1, October 1, November 1, and December 1.

What do you need to have with you?

- Your business goals.
- Your Quarterly High Level Networking Action Plan.
- Last month's Network with Intention check in. (Refer to last month's plan)

What are your top business goals for the month? _____

Recent networking wins: _____

Since last month, what are some positive results you have experienced? Referrals received? New connections made? New power partner relationships?

Recent networking lessons learned: _____

Since last month, what is a challenge you may have experienced in your networking? What can you learn from it? Some examples: You were counting on someone to assist you in a launch and their actions didn't match their words. Or a program you are part of is not yielding you the results you were hoping for.

Recommit to the number of new professionals you will connect with each day _____

Ask yourself, what new Power Partners (by name) do you want to build a relationship with this month?

1. _____

2. _____

3. _____

4. _____

Former Power Partners (by name) to reconnect with this month:

1. _____

2. _____

3. _____

4. _____

Content marketing themes to cover this month:

Monthly theme _____

Week 1 theme _____

Week 2 theme _____

Week 3 theme _____

Week 4 theme _____

Week 5 theme _____ (if needed)

Review networking calendars for upcoming events for this month.

Are there any new networking organizations you want to visit?
_____

Any specific events you plan to attend? _____

Organizations I'm a member of I will attend this month:
_____

This month's Big Asks.

Week 1 _____

Week 2 _____

Week 3 _____

Week 4 _____

Week 5 _____ (if needed)

Other notes:

You've covered so much ground. Congratulations! It's time for some closing thoughts.

ACTION STEPS:

Set dates on your calendar for your networking planning for the coming year.

Complete your quarterly Networking Action Plan.

Complete your monthly Networking with Intention Check In.

Repeat.

IN CLOSING

Can you imagine if they taught us high-level networking strategies in school how much farther ahead we would be in life and business?

Now that you know what you know, you can implement these strategies throughout the remainder of your business life—every time you change direction or release a new product or service, you have these tools available to help you create a steady stream of referrals.

What do you still need to complete?

- High Level Networking Assessment
- Business Commercial Blueprint
- Big ASK Brainstorm with up to 12 Big ASKs
- Power Partner Brainstorm with up to 12 Power Partners
- One-to-One Session Profile
- Signature Speech/Presentations

Be sure to mark your calendar to complete your:

- Networking Action Plan (Quarterly)
- Network with Intention Check In (Monthly)

I invite you to connect with me online:

- *Facebook*: terilee.harrison
- *LinkedIn: in/terilee*
- *Instagram: @terileeharrison*

Wishing you the very best as you expand your network!

Much success,

Terilee

ACKNOWLEDGMENTS

God: I am in absolute awe of the things you has done for me in my life. I pray I will use the talents you have given me throughout the remainder of my life to show others how they can find you.

Terry Harrison: I am so blessed you are my husband. I cannot put into words how much it means to me to have your full support of me doing the work I love. I don't take this (or you!) for granted. Thank you for sharing your editing gifts and talents on this project. I love you!

Kelli C. Holmes: It's been 15 years since we began working together at TEAM Referral Network and I told you, "I'll start a chapter or two." We've lived 5 minutes from each other, and we've lived almost 9,000 miles apart. Here's to another 15 years of doing the work we love and loyal friendship. I'm grateful for you and excited for what's to come!

Eric Lofholm: Since the day we met many years ago, I've always seen you as a powerful force of positivity and motivation to so many people—including me. I am beyond honored to teach and coach networking as part of ELI's offerings and look forward to serving many people with you over the coming years and help them become the best that they can be.

Chella Diaz: What a blessing it's been to be on the journey with you over the last several years. Your support of me, the Virtual TEAM community, and my networking coaching and training has been priceless. I am where I am today and on the road to where I am going thanks to you.

Bles Payawal: I am blessed to have you on my team. Thank you for your desire to support me at the highest level and your willingness to learn new things and take on any project I suggest (like this book, it's launch, my latest programs—the list is endless). You are appreciated. You are loved.

Armend Meha: Thank you for helping me create yet another cover for this latest book. Here's to working with you again in the future!

My Virtual TEAM members: I wish I could acknowledge each of you here by name. You are the reason I jump out of bed each and every morning excited to serve others. I see each of you and the extraordinary way you're showing up in the world. You inspire me!

Robbie Samuels: I'm so grateful we met (by referral. I appreciate you so openly sharing your book launch process with other authors. Timing was everything. When this book launches in a big way and reaches more people, it will be because off what I learned from you. Thank you.

The *High Level Networking* Book Launch Team: My sincere thanks goes to all those who took the time to read, review, and share *High Level Networking* with their business friends. I know how busy you all are. Your support means so much. Please stay in touch and let me know if I can reciprocate in any way!

ABOUT TERILEE HARRISON

Terilee Harrison is a virtual and face-to-face networking trainer/coach with *Eric Lofholm International*, an entrepreneur, a global speaker, and author.

She is passionate about helping coaches, consultants, and solopreneurs to network in the most dynamic and lucrative way.

An expert in business networking and relationship marketing, for 15 years, Terilee has worked with thousands of entrepreneurs at *TEAM Referral Network* in Southern California. After an international move from the US to Singapore in 2017, she went full force into virtual networking in 2018 and now serves business owners from around the world through the *TEAM Referral Network Virtual Chapters* global online referral community.

As a professional speaker, Terilee's ability to both inspire and challenge audiences to action and change can be attributed to her consistently authentic presentation regarding who she is, where she's been, and what she's learned along the way.

Terilee resides in Singapore with her husband, Terry. Together, they have four children and one granddaughter.

Connect with Terilee:

On Facebook: terilee.harrison

On LinkedIn: in/terilee

On Instagram: terileeharrison

Email **terilee@ericlofholm.com**

What's App +65 8118 1648

BOOK TERILEE

Terilee is available to speak to your sales team, networking organization, or your business event. She is a regular podcast and livestream guest and would love to talk about networking on your business-related podcast.

Some of Terilee's popular speaking topics are:

- Top Strategies to Boost Your Business Through Online Networking
- How to Create a Powerful One Minute Business Commercial that Gets Results!
- Grow Your Business with Ease by Leveraging Power Partner Relationships
- How to Instantly Leverage LinkedIn to Build Your Business Network

For more information, book a time to discuss your speaking needs at **www.bookterilee.com**.

TO LEARN MORE

If you liked what you learned in this book and you'd like to learn more, your next step is to sign up for my online networking training opportunities.

My ELITE Networking Training System is designed to provide you with everything you need to grow your business with ease:

- The **Connect+ 4-Week Online Bootcamp** will teach you how to create a steady stream of referrals.
- The **Content+ 90-Day Program** will teach you how to show up powerfully when you network. You *will* get your content published!
- The **Networking+ 12-Month Program** will focus on how to do the largest deals of your life.

You can learn more here: **www.terileeharrison.com**

Are you interested in growing your business nationally and globally with ease? It's easy when you join TEAM Referral Network Virtual Chapters' globally online referral community.

Wondering how you can you get involved?

✓ Visit one of our national/globally based weekly, exclusive category referral chapters! Find a day/time to visit here:
www.vteamnetwork.com

✓ Attend our twice monthly Global Gatherings featuring global online networking and outstanding speakers. Info/register:
www.vteamgathering.com

✓ Ready to join today for only $57 USD/month? Visit
www.joinvteam.com

Got questions? Email **terilee@teamreferralnetwork.com**

A REQUEST

Thank you for reading my book. I would love to hear from you!

Writing an Amazon review is as easy as answering any of these questions:

- Who would you recommend this book to?
- What is your most valuable takeaway or insight?
- What did you enjoy most about the book?
- What have you done differently—or what will you do differently—because of what you read?

A review can be just 2-3 sentences. Your feedback helps to get this book into the hands of those who need it the most.

I look forward to hearing about the referral and joint venture partnerships you created, how they helped to grow your business, and how your email list grows because of the action you took because of this book.

Best,

Terilee

Made in USA - Kendallville, IN
89096_9781948137195
09.01.2022 1345